Explore the U.S.A.

FLORIDA

Karen Durrie

www.av2books.com

LET'S READ

AV²
BY WEIGL™

ADDED VALUE • AUDIO VISUAL

Go to **www.av2books.com**, and enter this book's unique code.

BOOK CODE

N 4 2 4 2

AV² by Weigl brings you media enhanced books that support active learning.

AV² provides enriched content that supplements and complements this book. Weigl's AV² books strive to create inspired learning and engage young minds in a total learning experience.

Your AV² Media Enhanced books come alive with...

Audio
Listen to sections of the book read aloud.

Video
Watch informative video clips.

Embedded Weblinks
Gain additional information for research.

Try This!
Complete activities and hands-on experiments.

Key Words
Study vocabulary, and complete a matching word activity.

Quizzes
Test your knowledge.

Slide Show
View images and captions, and prepare a presentation.

... and much, much more!

Published by AV² by Weigl
350 5ᵗʰ Avenue, 59ᵗʰ Floor
New York, NY 10118
Website: www.av2books.com   www.weigl.com

Library of Congress Cataloging-in-Publication Data

Durrie, Karen.
 Florida / Karen Durrie.
   p. cm. -- (Explore the U.S.A.)
Includes bibliographical references and index.
ISBN 978-1-61913-339-6 (hard cover : alk. paper)
1. Florida--Juvenile literature. I. Title.
F311.5.D87 2012
975.9--dc23
                                        2012014761

Printed in the United States of America in North Mankato, Minnesota
1 2 3 4 5 6 7 8 9 16 15 14 13 12

052012
WEP040512

Project Coordinator: Karen Durrie
Art Director: Terry Paulhus

Weigl acknowledges Getty Images as the primary image supplier for this book.

2

FLORIDA

Contents

This is Florida.
It is called the Sunshine State.
Florida gets more than 200 days
of sunshine each year.

5

This is the shape of Florida. It is in the south part of the United States. Florida has water on three sides of the state.

Where is Florida?

Canada

United States

Pacific Ocean

Atlantic Ocean

Mexico

Gulf of Mexico

Florida borders two states, the Atlantic Ocean, and the Gulf of Mexico.

Explorers from Spain came to Florida almost 500 years ago. Their ships landed on the north coast.

The name Florida is a Spanish word that means "full of flowers."

The orange blossom is the Florida state flower. It grows on orange trees.

The state seal has a woman, a steamboat, and a palm tree.

The woman is a Seminole Indian.

This is the state flag of Florida. It is red and white with the Florida seal in the middle.

The red X comes from an older flag.

13

The state animal of Florida is the panther. A panther is a big cat. Panthers can purr, roar, and even whistle.

There are only about 100 Florida panthers left in nature.

This is the capital of Florida.
It is called Tallahassee.
Tallahassee means
"old fields."

Manatees live in rivers
near Tallahassee.

Oranges grow in Florida.
Florida oranges are sold
all over the world. Oranges
can be used to make juice.

About 900 million gallons
of juice are made from
Florida oranges each year.

Florida is known for its beautiful beaches and fun parks.

People come to enjoy the warm weather in Florida.

FLORIDA FACTS

These pages provide detailed information that expands on the interesting facts found in the book. These pages are intended to be used by adults as a learning support to help young readers round out their knowledge of each state in the *Explore the U.S.A.* series.

Pages 4–5

Florida is one of the southernmost states. The state experiences 220 to 260 sunny days each year, although this varies from year to year and city to city. Florida's subtropical climate is one reason it is the warmest state in the country on average. Tourism is one of Florida's biggest industries. In 2010, more than 80 million tourists visited Florida.

Pages 6–7

On March 3, 1845, Florida was the 27th state to join the United States. Florida is on a peninsula that separates the Gulf of Mexico from the Atlantic Ocean. To the north, Florida shares its only land borders with Georgia and Alabama. The islands off the southern tip of Florida are called keys. This comes from the Spanish *cayo*, meaning "little island."

Pages 8–9

Ponce de Leon was the first Spanish explorer to come to Florida. He landed near present-day St. Augustine in April 1513. He called the area *la Florida* after the Spanish Easter celebration *Pascua Florida*, which means "feast of the flowers." Pascua Florida Day is celebrated in the state every April 2. This day celebrates de Leon's discovery.

Pages 10–11

The state flower signifies the importance of the orange industry to Florida. More than 6 million tons (5.4 million tonnes) of oranges are produced in Florida each year. The steamboat on the state seal represents commerce. The seal was changed in 1985 to correct several errors. The former seal depicted a Western Plains Indian, which was revised to a Seminole Indian.

Pages 12–13

The red bars on the Florida state flag are known as the Cross of St. Andrews. This cross was taken from the Confederate flag. It represents Florida's participation in the American Civil War. The design was approved in 1900.

Pages 14–15

The panther was selected to be the Florida state animal in 1982. The state government asked students to choose from different animals that were common to the state. Panthers live in the marshlands of Florida. The Florida panther is an endangered species. It has lost much of its habitat to the state's growing human population.

Pages 16–17

The word *Tallahassee* comes from an Apalachee Indian word meaning "old fields." Each winter, manatees migrate to a state park near Tallahassee. Manatees are aquatic mammals. They are found in shallow rivers, bays, and coastal areas. Manatees are endangered. Collisions with boats are one of the main threats to manatee survival.

Pages 18–19

Oranges grow in Florida from November to April. There are many kinds of oranges. Some are good for eating, while others are better suited to making juice. Navel oranges are an example of a good eating orange. About 70 percent of all oranges sold in the United States are grown in Florida.

Pages 20–21

Florida has 1,197 miles (1,926 kilometers) of coastline. Swamps and marshes make up much of Florida's coastline, along with 663 miles (1,067 km) of beaches. One of the most famous beaches in Florida is Daytona Beach. Many theme parks are found in the state, including Disney World and Sea World in Orlando.

KEY WORDS

Research has shown that as much as 65 percent of all written material published in English is made up of 300 words. These 300 words cannot be taught using pictures or learned by sounding them out. They must be recognized by sight. This book contains 63 common sight words to help young readers improve their reading fluency and comprehension. This book also teaches young readers several important content words, such as proper nouns. These words are paired with pictures to aid in learning and improve understanding.

Page	Sight Words First Appearance
4	each, days, gets, is, it, more, of, state, than, the, this, year
7	and, has, in, on, part, sides, three, two, water, where
8	a, almost, came, from, means, name, that, their, to, word, years
11	grows, Indian, trees
12	an, comes, white, with
15	about, animal, are, big, can, even, left, only, there
16	live, near, old, rivers
19	all, be, made, make, over, used, world
21	for, its, people

Page	Content Words First Appearance
4	Florida, sunshine
7	Atlantic Ocean, Gulf of Mexico, shape, United States
8	coast, explorers, flowers, ships, Spain
11	orange blossom, seal, steamboat, woman
12	flag, middle
15	cat, nature, panther
16	capital, manatees, Tallahassee
19	gallons, juice, oranges
21	beaches, parks, weather

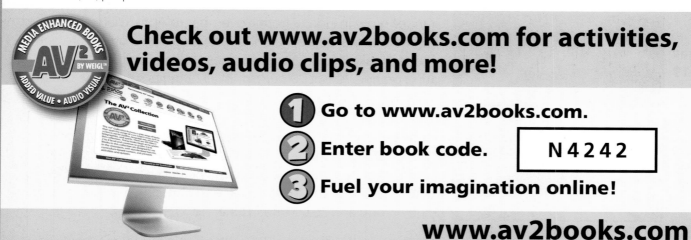

contents

Dear Friends,

You and your family are hungry . . . but there's so little time to cook. Whether working inside or outside of the home, everyone's busy. But that doesn't mean you have to sacrifice good food. With this great collection of delicious, healthful and most important, easy recipes, Betty Crocker makes cooking for the family so simple!

Do you cook the same meals for your family over and over again? Here are over 150 recipes to help you break out of that rut! Retire those tired appetizers and impress friends and family by serving inventive small bites like Margarita Shrimp Cocktail and Chipotle Cheesecake. Whether you serve them as sides or main dishes, your family will surely savor scrumptious salads and soups like Grilled Chicken Satay Salad and Italian Tomato Soup with Pesto-Cheese Toasts. Versatile sandwich and pizza dishes like Chicken BLT Sandwiches and Double-Cheese, Spinach and Chicken Pizza will quickly become family favorites. You'll find the best of both worlds—healthy and delicious foods—with main dishes like Zesty Roasted Chicken and Potatoes and Lemon and Herb Salmon Packets. Grilling season will never be the same once you serve Ginger-Lime Tuna Steaks and Chicken with Oregano-Peach Sauce—dishes that go far beyond the usual grilling staples, hamburgers and hot dogs. And don't worry. Recipes like Four-Cheese Mashed Potato Casserole and Mini Meat Loaves will help satisfy the occasional craving for comfort food. Last but not least, delectable desserts like Dark Chocolate Raspberry Fondue and Tiny Lemon Gem Tarts will delight the sweet-tooth in your family.

So next time you feel tempted to grab a take-out menu, reach for this book instead!

Regards,

olive and herb deviled eggs

Prep Time: 1 hr ▪ **Start to Finish:** 1 hr ▪ 16 Deviled Eggs

8 eggs
¹/₃ cup mayonnaise or salad dressing
2 tablespoons finely chopped parsley
2 tablespoons finely chopped fresh marjoram leaves
2 tablespoons finely chopped fresh chives
¹/₂ teaspoon garlic-pepper blend
¹/₂ cup chopped ripe olives
8 pitted ripe olives
Fresh parsley or marjoram sprigs or leaves, if desired

1 In 3-quart saucepan, place eggs in single layer; add enough cold water to cover eggs by 1 inch. Cover; heat to boiling. Remove from heat; let stand covered 15 minutes. Drain. Immediately place eggs in cold water with ice cubes or run cold water over eggs until completely cooled.

2 To remove shell from each egg, crackle it by tapping gently all over; roll between hands to loosen. Peel, starting at large end. With rippled vegetable cutter or sharp knife, cut each egg in half lengthwise. Carefully remove yolks and place in small bowl; mash with fork. Reserve egg white halves.

3 Stir mayonnaise, chopped herbs, garlic-pepper blend and chopped olives into mashed yolks. Carefully spoon mixture into egg white halves, mounding lightly.

4 Cut whole pitted olives into slices; top each egg half with olive slices. Garnish with small herb sprigs or leaves.

1 Deviled Egg: Calories 80 (Calories from Fat 60); Total Fat 7g (Saturated Fat 1.5g); Cholesterol 110mg; Sodium 110mg; Total Carbohydrate 0g (Dietary Fiber 0g); Protein 3g

Instead of an olive slice, top each egg half with a cherry tomato wedge. To make ahead, store stuffed eggs tightly covered in the fridge up to 24 hours before serving.

ham salad in cucumber cups

Prep Time: 20 min ▪ **Start to Finish:** 20 min ▪ 24 Appetizers

2 seedless cucumbers
³/₄ cup ham salad
4 lemon slices, cut into wedges, if desired

1 Cut tapered ends from cucumbers. Peel lengthwise strips of peel every half inch with citrus stripper. Cut cucumbers into ⁵/₈- to ³/₄-inch slices. Make indentation in center of each slice, without going all the way through, by scooping with small melon ball cutter.

2 Fill each indentation with about 1 teaspoon ham salad. Top each appetizer with lemon wedge.

1 Appetizer: Calories 15 (Calories from Fat 10); Total Fat 1g (Saturated Fat 0g); Cholesterol 0mg; Sodium 50mg; Total Carbohydrate 0g (Dietary Fiber 0g); Protein 0g

double cheese bruschetta

Prep Time: 15 min ■ **Start to Finish:** 15 min ■ 18 Appetizers

2 oz feta cheese, crumbled (¹/₂ cup)
1 package (3 oz) cream cheese, softened
18 toasted baguette slices, about ¹/₄ inch thick
18 marinated kalamata or Greek olives, pitted, sliced
9 cherry tomatoes, sliced

1 In small bowl, mix feta cheese and cream cheese; spread on baguette slices.

2 Top with olives and tomatoes.

Sun-Dried Tomato Bruschetta: Spread cream cheese on toasted bread. Top with julienne strips of sun-dried tomatoes packed in oil and herbs, drained. Sprinkle with toasted pine nuts.

Mascarpone Bruschetta: Spread mascarpone cheese on toasted bread. Top with dried cranberries, crumbled dried rosemary leaves and a dash of ground cardamom.

1 Appetizer: Calories 55 (Calories from Fat 25); Total Fat 3g (Saturated Fat 2g); Cholesterol 10mg; Sodium 130mg; Total Carbohydrate 5g (Dietary Fiber 0g); Protein 2g

Double Cheese Bruschetta (left) and
Mascarpone Bruschetta (right)

chipotle cheesecake

Prep Time: 20 min ▪ **Start to Finish:** 5 hr 5 min ▪ 36 Servings

1 cup crushed tortilla chips

3 tablespoons butter or margarine, melted

2 packages (8 oz each) cream cheese, softened

2 eggs

$^1/_2$ cup sour cream

2 cups shredded Colby–Monterey Jack cheese blend (8 oz)

$^1/_4$ cup chopped drained roasted red bell peppers (from 7-oz jar)

4 chipotle chiles in adobo sauce (from 7-oz can), seeded, chopped (2 tablespoons)

1 tablespoon adobo sauce from can of chipotle chiles

Large tortilla chips, if desired

1 Heat oven to 375°F. In medium bowl, mix tortilla chips and butter until well blended. Press evenly in bottom of springform pan, 9×3 inches. Bake about 8 minutes or until golden brown.

2 Reduce oven temperature to 325°F. In large bowl, beat cream cheese with electric mixer on medium speed until smooth. Add eggs; beat until well blended. Beat in sour cream. Stir in cheese, bell peppers, chipotle chiles and adobo sauce until well blended. Spoon evenly over crust.

3 Bake uncovered 40 to 45 minutes or until center is set. Run knife around edge of cheesecake to loosen. Cool completely at room temperature, about 2 hours. Cover and refrigerate at least 2 hours but no longer than 24 hours. Remove side of pan. Serve cheesecake with tortilla chips.

1 Serving: Calories 100 (Calories from Fat 80); Total Fat 9g (Saturated Fat 5g); Cholesterol 35mg; Sodium 125mg; Total Carbohydrate 2g (Dietary Fiber 0g); Protein 3g

Make it easy for your guests to help themselves to this savory cheesecake from your appetizer buffet. Cut a 4-inch diameter circle in the center of the cheesecake before cutting it into wedges so guests can easily cut short wedges from 2 rings of cheesecake instead of longer wedges.

salmon-pimiento appetizers

Prep Time: 15 min ■ **Start to Finish:** 15 min ■ 16 Appetizers

1 package (4.5 oz) smoked salmon (hot-smoked), skin removed, flaked

¹/₃ cup pimiento cheese spread (from 5-oz jar)

2 teaspoons mayonnaise or salad dressing

2 medium green onions, thinly sliced (2 tablespoons)

¹/₈ teaspoon pepper

16 slices cocktail pumpernickel bread

16 thin slices seedless cucumber

2 tablespoons tiny dill weed sprigs

1 In medium bowl, mix salmon, cheese spread, mayonnaise, onions and pepper. Spread evenly on bread slices.

2 Cut cucumber slices in half almost to edge and twist; place on salmon mixture. Garnish with dill weed sprigs.

1 Appetizer: Calories 45 (Calories from Fat 20); Total Fat 2g (Saturated Fat 1g); Cholesterol 5mg; Sodium 150mg; Total Carbohydrate 4g (Dietary Fiber 0g); Protein 3g

Can't find smoked salmon? Use a 6-oz can of boneless skinless salmon, drained, instead.

cheesy apple polenta bites

Prep Time: 35 min ▪ **Start to Finish:** 12 hr 55 min ▪ 72 Appetizers

1 cup yellow cornmeal

1 cup cold water

2³/₄ cups boiling water

1 teaspoon salt

2 tablespoons grated onion

1 tablespoon chopped fresh or

    1 teaspoon dried sage leaves

1 cup shredded Cheddar cheese (4 oz)

1 small unpeeled apple

Juice of 1 medium lemon (2 to 3 tablespoons)

1 Line 8-inch square glass (2-quart) baking dish with foil, leaving 1 inch of foil overhanging at 2 opposite sides of dish; grease foil. In 2-quart saucepan, mix cornmeal and cold water. Stir in boiling water and salt. Cook about 5 minutes, stirring constantly, until mixture boils and thickens; reduce heat to low. Stir in onion, sage and ¹/₂ cup of the cheese. Cook uncovered 5 minutes, stirring occasionally; remove from heat.

2 Spread cornmeal mixture (polenta) in baking dish. Cover and refrigerate at least 12 hours until firm.

3 Heat oven to 400°F. Grease 15×10×1-inch pan. Remove polenta from baking dish, using foil edges to lift. Cut polenta into 6 rows by 6 rows to make 36 squares. Cut each square diagonally to make 2 triangles; place in pan. Bake uncovered about 15 minutes or until golden brown.

4 Cut apple into thin slices. Cut slices into fourths. Dip apple pieces into lemon juice to keep them from discoloring. Top each triangle with 1 apple piece. Sprinkle remaining ¹/₂ cup cheese over apple pieces. Bake about 5 minutes or until cheese is melted. Serve warm.

1 Appetizer: Calories 20 (Calories from Fat 10); Total Fat 1g (Saturated Fat 0g); Cholesterol 0mg; Sodium 40mg; Total Carbohydrate 2g (Dietary Fiber 0g); Protein 1g.

Save time! Use purchased polenta, and eliminate the preparation time. Simply slice the polenta, cut the slices into fourths and bake as directed.

fireside popovers with brie

Prep Time: 10 min ■ **Start to Finish:** 30 min ■ 24 Popovers

2 eggs
1 cup all-purpose flour
1 cup milk
1 teaspoon sugar
1/2 teaspoon salt
1/2 lb Brie cheese, cut into 24 chunks

1 Heat oven to 450°F. Generously grease 24 mini muffin cups. In medium bowl, beat eggs slightly with fork or whisk. Beat in flour, milk, sugar and salt just until smooth (do not overbeat). Divide batter evenly among muffin cups. Bake 5 minutes.

2 Reduce oven temperature to 350°F. Bake about 10 minutes longer or until crusty and golden brown. Cut a small slit in top of each popover. Insert cheese chunk in each popover. Bake 5 minutes. Immediately remove from pan. Serve hot.

Do Ahead: Bake popovers and cut the slit in top of each. Cool, wrap tightly and freeze. When ready to serve, insert cheese chunk in each frozen popover. Place in muffin cups. Heat in 350°F oven 8 to 10 minutes or until cheese is melted.

1 Popover: Calories 60 (Calories from Fat 25); Total Fat 3g (Saturated Fat 2g); Cholesterol 25mg; Sodium 140mg; Total Carbohydrate 5g (Dietary Fiber 0g); Protein 3g

If desired, serve with apple wedges and sprigs.

basil cheese triangles

Prep Time: 25 min ▪ **Start to Finish:** 40 min ▪ 72 Triangles

1 lb feta cheese

2 eggs, slightly beaten

$1/4$ cup finely chopped fresh or 1 tablespoon dried basil leaves

$1/4$ teaspoon white pepper

1 package (16 oz) frozen phyllo (filo) pastry sheets (18×14 inch), thawed

$1/3$ cup butter or margarine, melted

1 Heat oven to 400°F. Grease cookie sheet. In small bowl, crumble cheese; mash with fork. Stir in eggs, basil and white pepper until well mixed.

2 Cut phyllo sheets lengthwise into 2-inch strips. Cover with plastic wrap, then with damp towel to keep them from drying out. Place 1 level teaspoon cheese mixture on end of 1 strip. Fold strip over cheese mixture, end over end in triangular shape, to opposite end. Place on cookie sheet. Repeat with remaining strips and cheese mixture. Brush triangles lightly with butter.

3 Bake 12 to 15 minutes or until puffed and golden brown. Serve warm.

Do Ahead: Cover and refrigerate unbaked triangles up to 24 hours before baking; bake as directed. Or freeze tightly covered up to 2 months; increase bake time by 5 minutes.

1 Triangle: Calories 45 (Calories from Fat 20); Total Fat 3g (Saturated Fat 1g); Cholesterol 10mg; Sodium 105mg; Total Carbohydrate 4g (Dietary Fiber 0g); Protein 2g

dill havarti–shrimp appetizers

Prep Time: 20 min ■ **Start to Finish:** 20 min ■ 24 Appetizers

24 pumpernickel cocktail bread slices

3 tablespoons Dijon mustard

1 tablespoon honey

6 slices (about 8 oz) dill Havarti cheese

24 cooked deveined peeled medium or large shrimp, thawed if frozen, tail shells removed

2 tablespoons finely chopped red bell pepper

2 tablespoons chopped fresh dill weed

1 Heat oven to 400°F. Place bread slices in ungreased 15×10×1-inch pan. Bake 4 to 6 minutes or until crisp.

2 In small bowl, mix mustard and honey; spread over bread slices. Cut cheese into 2-inch squares. Top each bread slice with cheese, shrimp and bell pepper. Sprinkle with dill weed.

3 Bake 3 to 5 minutes or until cheese is melted.

1 Appetizer: Calories 70 (Calories from Fat 35); Total Fat 4g (Saturated Fat 2g); Cholesterol 20mg; Sodium 180mg; Total Carbohydrate 4g (Dietary Fiber 0g); Protein 4g

If you can't find the dill-flavored Havarti, you can use regular Havarti, or you might try Gouda for a flavor change.

brie quesadillas with mango guacamole

Prep Time: 35 min ▪ **Start to Finish:** 35 min ▪ 24 Servings

Guacamole

1 medium avocado, pitted, peeled and quartered

$^1/_2$ small jalapeño chile, seeded, finely chopped

1 small clove garlic, finely chopped

2 tablespoons lime juice

$^1/_4$ cup chopped fresh cilantro

$^1/_8$ teaspoon salt

$^1/_2$ medium mango, cut in half lengthwise, seed
   removed, peeled and diced

Quesadillas

6 flour tortillas (8 inch)

1 round (6 to 7 oz) Brie cheese, cut into $^1/_8$-inch
   strips (not wedges)

$^1/_4$ lb thinly sliced cooked ham (from deli)

1 tablespoon vegetable oil

1 In food processor, place all guacamole ingredients except mango. Cover; process, using 3 or 4 quick on-and-off motions until coarsely chopped. Place in small bowl; stir in mango. Set aside.

2 Top half of each tortilla with cheese and ham. Fold tortilla over and press down. Brush top with oil.

3 Heat 12-inch skillet over medium-high heat. Place 3 quesadillas, oil side down, in skillet. Brush tops with half of remaining oil. Cook 2 to 3 minutes, turning once, until both sides are golden brown and cheese is melted. Repeat with remaining quesadillas and oil. Cut each into 4 wedges. Serve with guacamole.

1 Serving: Calories 80 (Calories from Fat 45); Total Fat 5g (Saturated Fat 2g); Cholesterol 10mg; Sodium 190mg; Total Carbohydrate 7g (Dietary Fiber 0g); Protein 3g

If you prefer, you can mash the guacamole ingredients with a fork instead of using a food processor.

corn and crab quesadillas

Prep Time: 15 min ■ **Start to Finish:** 15 min ■ 18 Wedges

1 package (8 oz) cream cheese, softened

1 can (11 oz) whole kernel corn, drained

¹/₂ cup chopped fresh cilantro or parsley

5 medium green onions, chopped (¹/₃ cup)

1 jar (2 oz) diced pimientos, drained

¹/₂ teaspoon black pepper

¹/₄ teaspoon ground red pepper (cayenne)

1 lb chopped cooked crabmeat or imitation crabmeat (2 cups)

6 sun-dried tomato or spinach-cilantro flavored flour tortillas (8 to 10 inch)

1 tablespoon butter or margarine, melted

1 In medium bowl, mix cream cheese, corn, cilantro, onions, pimientos, black pepper and red pepper. Fold in crabmeat. Spread ²/₃ cup of the crabmeat mixture over each tortilla; fold tortilla in half, pressing lightly. Brush butter over both sides of each tortilla.

2 In 12-inch skillet, cook 3 tortillas at a time over medium-high heat about 5 minutes, turning once, until light brown. Cut each quesadilla into 3 wedges.

1 Wedge: Calories 140 (Calories from Fat 65); Total Fat 7g (Saturated Fat 4g); Cholesterol 40mg; Sodium 220mg; Total Carbohydrate 12g (Dietary Fiber 1g); Protein 8g

Instead of pimientos, you can substitute roasted red bell peppers, available in jars, drained and chopped, or chopped fresh red bell pepper.

black bean and corn wonton cups

Prep Time: 25 min ▪ **Start to Finish:** 35 min ▪ 36 Appetizers

36 wonton skins

$^2/_3$ cup chunky-style salsa

$^1/_4$ cup chopped fresh cilantro

$^1/_2$ teaspoon ground cumin

$^1/_2$ teaspoon chili powder

1 can (15.25 oz) whole kernel corn, drained

1 can (15 oz) black beans, rinsed, drained

$^1/_4$ cup plus 2 tablespoons sour cream

Cilantro sprigs, if desired

1 Heat oven to 350°F. Gently fit 1 wonton skin into each of 36 mini muffin cups, pressing against bottom and side. Bake 8 to 10 minutes or until light golden brown. Remove from pan; cool on cooling rack.

2 Mix remaining ingredients except sour cream and cilantro sprigs. Just before serving, spoon bean mixture into wonton cups. Top each with $^1/_2$ teaspoon sour cream. Garnish each with cilantro sprig.

1 Appetizer: Calories 55 (Calories from Fat 10); Total Fat 1g (Saturated Fat 0g); Cholesterol 5mg; Sodium 90mg; Total Carbohydrate 10g (Dietary Fiber 1g); Protein 2g

empanadillas

Prep Time: 40 min ■ **Start to Finish:** 1 hr 5 min ■ 24 Empanadillas

8 oz bulk spicy pork sausage

1 medium onion, finely chopped ($^1/_2$ cup)

1 teaspoon finely chopped garlic

$^1/_4$ cup raisins, finely chopped

$^1/_4$ cup pitted green olives, finely chopped

1 teaspoon ground cumin

1 package (17.3 oz) frozen puff pastry sheets, thawed

1 egg

1 teaspoon water

Fresh cilantro, if desired

1 Heat oven to 400°F. Line large cookie sheet with foil or cooking parchment paper; lightly spray with cooking spray.

2 In 10-inch skillet, cook sausage, onion and garlic over medium-high heat 5 to 7 minutes, stirring occasionally, until sausage is no longer pink. Stir in raisins, olives and cumin; remove from heat.

3 On lightly floured surface, roll 1 sheet of pastry into 12×9-inch rectangle, trimming edges if necessary. Cut into twelve 3-inch squares.

4 Place 1 tablespoon sausage mixture on each pastry square. In small bowl, beat egg and water with fork until well blended. Brush egg mixture on edges of pastry squares. Fold pastry over filling to make triangles; press edges with fork to seal. Place on cookie sheet. Repeat with remaining pastry and sausage mixture. Brush tops of triangles with egg mixture.

5 Bake 20 to 25 minutes or until golden brown. Serve warm. Garnish with cilantro.

1 Empanadilla: Calories 140 (Calories from Fat 90); Total Fat 10g (Saturated Fat 3.5g); Cholesterol 35mg; Sodium 110mg; Total Carbohydrate 11g (Dietary Fiber 0g); Protein 3g

For a less spicy version, substitute round beef or ground turkey for the sausage.

smoked salmon puffs

Prep Time: 15 min ■ **Start to Finish:** 40 min ■ 24 Puffs

$^1/_2$ **cup Original Bisquick® mix**

$^1/_2$ **cup milk**

$^1/_4$ **cup sour cream**

$^1/_2$ **teaspoon Worcestershire sauce**

2 eggs

$^2/_3$ **cup shredded Cheddar cheese**

$^1/_3$ **cup chopped smoked salmon**

2 medium green onions, sliced (2 tablespoons)

1 Heat oven to 400°F. Spray 24 mini muffin cups with cooking spray.

2 In small bowl, beat Bisquick mix, milk, sour cream, Worcestershire sauce and eggs with fork until blended. Stir in remaining ingredients. Spoon about 1 tablespoon mixture into each muffin cup.

3 Bake 15 to 20 minutes or until golden. Cool 5 minutes. Loosen sides of puffs from pan; remove from pan. Serve warm.

1 Puff: Calories 40 (Calories from Fat 20); Total Fat 2.5g (Saturated Fat 1g); Cholesterol 25mg; Sodium 80mg; Total Carbohydrate 2g (Dietary Fiber 0g); Protein 2g

Try other flavors! Havarti, Colby, mozzarella or Monterey Jack cheese would all be delicious.

crab bites

Prep Time: 15 min ▪ **Start to Finish:** 40 min ▪ 45 Appetizers

³/₄ cup mayonnaise or salad dressing

³/₄ cup grated Parmesan cheese

¹/₂ teaspoon finely chopped garlic

8 medium green onions, finely chopped (¹/₂ cup)

1 can (14 oz) artichoke hearts, drained, diced

1 package (6 oz) ready-to-eat crabmeat, flaked

3 packages (2.1 oz each) frozen mini fillo dough shells (15 shells each), thawed

1 Heat oven to 375°F. Line cookie sheet with foil or cooking parchment paper.

2 In large bowl, mix all ingredients except fillo shells with spoon about 2 minutes or until well blended.

3 Place fillo shells on cookie sheet. Fill each shell with about 1 tablespoon crab mixture. Bake 20 to 25 minutes or until shells are puffed and golden brown. Serve warm.

1 Appetizer: Calories 50 (Calories from Fat 30); Total Fat 3.5g (Saturated Fat 0.5g); Cholesterol 5mg; Sodium 85mg; Total Carbohydrate 3g (Dietary Fiber 0g); Protein 2g

Add a little color! Garnish each crab bite with half of a cherry tomato.

margarita shrimp cocktail

Prep Time: 25 min ■ **Start to Finish:** 2 hrs 30 min ■ About 26 Shrimp

Shrimp
1¹/₂ lb medium shrimp with shells (26 to 30 shrimp)

4 cups water

2 teaspoons salt

1¹/₂ cups dry white wine or nonalcoholic wine

2 tablespoons lime juice

5 black peppercorns

Handful of fresh cilantro

Sauce
¹/₂ cup orange juice

¹/₂ cup ketchup

¹/₄ cup chopped fresh cilantro

¹/₄ cup lime juice

¹/₄ cup lemon juice

2 tablespoons tequila, if desired

2 tablespoons vegetable oil

¹/₂ teaspoon salt

¹/₈ teaspoon freshly ground pepper

Dash of red pepper sauce

1 Peel shrimp, leaving tails intact; reserve shells. Using a small, pointed knife or shrimp deveiner, make shallow cut lengthwise down back of each shrimp, then wash out the vein.

2 In 4-quart Dutch oven, heat shrimp shells, water and 2 teaspoons salt to boiling over high heat. Add wine, 2 tablespoons lime juice, the peppercorns and cilantro. Reduce heat to medium. Cover and cook 30 minutes.

3 Strain stock into large bowl and discard shells, peppercorns and cilantro. Return stock to Dutch oven and heat to boiling over high heat. Add shrimp; remove Dutch oven from heat. Cover and let stand 8 to 10 minutes until shrimp are pink and firm.

4 Meanwhile, fill large bowl half full with ice and water. When shrimp are done, remove from Dutch oven and plunge into ice bath to chill. (Reserve stock for another purpose, if desired.)

5 In medium nonreactive bowl, mix all sauce ingredients. Stir in cooked shrimp to coat. Cover and refrigerate at least 30 minutes but no longer than 3 hours. Serve cold.

1 Shrimp: Calories 30 (Calories from Fat 10); Total Fat 1g (Saturated Fat 0g); Cholesterol 25mg; Sodium 170mg; Total Carbohydrate 2g (Dietary Fiber 0g); Protein 3g

baked coconut shrimp

Prep Time: 30 min ■ **Start to Finish:** 40 min ■ About 31 Servings

³/₄ **cup apricot preserves**

2 tablespoons lime juice

¹/₂ **teaspoon ground mustard**

¹/₄ **cup all-purpose flour**

2 tablespoons packed brown sugar

¹/₄ **teaspoon salt**

Dash ground red pepper (cayenne)

1 egg

1 cup shredded coconut

1 lb uncooked deveined peeled medium (31 to 35 count) shrimp, thawed if frozen

2 tablespoons butter or margarine, melted

1 In 1-quart saucepan, mix apricot preserves, 1 tablespoon of the lime juice and the mustard. Cook over low heat, stirring occasionally, just until preserves are melted. Refrigerate while making shrimp.

2 Move oven rack to lowest position; heat oven to 425°F. Spray rack in broiler pan with cooking spray.

3 In shallow bowl, mix flour, brown sugar, salt and red pepper. In another shallow bowl, beat egg and remaining 1 tablespoon lime juice. In third shallow bowl, place coconut.

4 Coat each shrimp with flour mixture, then dip each side into egg mixture and coat well with coconut. Place on rack in broiler pan. Drizzle with butter.

5 Bake 7 to 8 minutes or until shrimp are pink and firm and coating is beginning to brown. Serve with preserves mixture.

Do Ahead: If you have time, coat the shrimp up to 2 hours ahead of time. Refrigerate covered, and bake just before serving.

1 Serving (1 shrimp and 1 teaspoon sauce): Calories 60 (Calories from Fat 20); Total Fat 2g (Saturated Fat 1.5g); Cholesterol 30mg; Sodium 60mg; Total Carbohydrate 8g (Dietary Fiber 0g); Protein 3g

spicy thai chicken wings

Prep Time: 25 min ▪ **Start to Finish:** 2 hr 15 min ▪ 40 Appetizers

20 chicken wings or drummettes (about 4 lb)

$^1/_4$ cup dry sherry or chicken broth

$^1/_4$ cup oyster sauce

$^1/_4$ cup honey

3 tablespoons chopped fresh cilantro

2 tablespoons chili sauce

2 tablespoons grated lime peel

4 medium green onions, chopped ($^1/_4$ cup)

3 cloves garlic, finely chopped

1 Cut each chicken wing at joints to make 3 pieces; discard tip. Cut off and discard excess skin.

2 In resealable heavy-duty food-storage plastic bag or large glass bowl, mix remaining ingredients. Add chicken to marinade. Seal bag; turn to coat. Refrigerate at least 1 hour but no longer than 24 hours, turning once.

3 Heat oven to 375°F. Place chicken in ungreased 15×10×1-inch pan. Bake uncovered 30 minutes, stirring frequently. Bake about 20 minutes longer or until juice of chicken is clear when thickest part is cut to bone.

1 Appetizer: Calories 60 (Calories from Fat 25); Total Fat 3g (Saturated Fat 1g); Cholesterol 15mg; Sodium 50mg; Total Carbohydrate 2g (Dietary Fiber 0g); Protein 5g

No oyster sauce? You can use 2 tablespoons of soy sauce instead; you can also use chicken broth instead of the sherry.

maple chicken drummettes

Prep Time: 15 min ∎ **Start to Finish:** 1 hr 10 min ∎ 20 Drummettes

$1/4$ **cup real maple syrup or honey**

$1/4$ **cup chili sauce**

2 tablespoons chopped fresh chives

1 tablespoon soy sauce

$1/2$ **teaspoon ground mustard**

$1/4$ **teaspoon ground red pepper (cayenne), if desired**

2 lb chicken drummettes (about 20)

1 Heat oven to 375°F. Mix all ingredients except chicken. Place chicken in ungreased 15×10×1-inch pan. Brush chicken with syrup mixture; turn chicken to coat.

2 Bake uncovered 45 to 55 minutes, turning once and brushing with sauce after 30 minutes, until juice of chicken is clear when thickest part is cut to bone.

1 Drummette: Calories 60 (Calories from Fat 20); Total Fat 2g (Saturated Fat 1g); Cholesterol 20mg; Sodium 100mg; Total Carbohydrate 4g (Dietary Fiber 0g); Protein 6g

For extra flavor, you can marinate the drummettes in the maple syrup mixture in a resealable food-storage plastic bag in the refrigerator for up to 1 hour. Then, just bake as directed.

If desired, sprinkle with crumbled blue cheese and garnish with chives.

honey mustard chicken tidbits

Prep Time: 15 min ▪ **Start to Finish:** 40 min ▪ 25 Servings

¹/₄ **cup honey mustard**
3 tablespoons butter or margarine
1 teaspoon garlic salt
³/₄ **cup garlic herb dry bread crumbs**
1 lb chicken breast tenders (not breaded), cut into 1-inch pieces (about 50 pieces)
Additional honey mustard, if desired

1 Heat oven to 400°F. Line cookie sheet with foil or cooking parchment paper; spray foil or paper with cooking spray.

2 In medium microwavable bowl, mix ¹/₄ cup honey mustard, the butter and garlic salt. Microwave uncovered on High 45 to 60 seconds or until butter is melted.

3 Place bread crumbs in large resealable food-storage plastic bag. Add chicken pieces to mustard mixture; stir to coat. Shake chicken pieces in bag of bread crumbs until coated. Place on cookie sheet. Discard any remaining honey mustard and bread crumbs.

4 Bake 20 to 25 minutes or until chicken is no longer pink in center. Serve with additional honey mustard.

Do Ahead: Coat the chicken pieces 2 to 3 hours before baking, then cover and refrigerate until it's time to bake them.

1 Serving (2 pieces): Calories 70 (Calories from Fat 35); Total Fat 4g (Saturated Fat 1g); Cholesterol 15mg; Sodium 130mg; Total Carbohydrate 3g (Dietary Fiber 0g); Protein 5g

chicken-ham bites

Prep Time: 30 min ∎ **Start to Finish:** 1 hr 15 min ∎ 36 Appetizers

2 boneless skinless chicken breasts, cut into $1/2$- to $3/4$-inch pieces (36 pieces)
$1/2$ cup Italian dressing
14 to 16 cremini mushrooms, cut into $1/4$-inch slices
6 oz sliced cooked deli ham, cut into 1-inch-wide strips
4 fresh basil leaves, finely sliced

1 In shallow bowl, place chicken pieces. Pour dressing over chicken. Cover and refrigerate 30 minutes to marinate.

2 Heat oven to 425°F. Line 15×10×1-inch pan with foil. Spray foil with cooking spray. Place 1 chicken piece on each mushroom slice; wrap with ham strip. Place seam side down (mushroom on bottom) in pan. Drizzle with remaining marinade in bowl.

3 Bake 10 to 12 minutes or until chicken is no longer pink in center. Place basil on top of each bite. Serve with cocktail toothpicks if desired.

Do Ahead: Bake these tasty appetizers up to 24 hours in advance. Transfer them to an ovenproof baking dish; cover and refrigerate. When ready to serve, reheat at 350°F for 20 to 25 minutes.

1 Appetizer: Calories 35 (Calories from Fat 20); Total Fat 2g (Saturated Fat 0g); Cholesterol 5mg; Sodium 90mg; Total Carbohydrate 1g (Dietary Fiber 0g); Protein 3g

bacon-turkey bites

Prep Time: 25 min ∎ **Start to Finish:** 1 hr 10 min ∎ 24 to 30 Appetizers

1 small turkey breast tenderloin ($^1/_2$ to $^3/_4$ lb), cut into $^1/_2$- to $^3/_4$-inch cubes

$^1/_2$ cup honey mustard dressing

8 to 10 slices bacon, cut crosswise into thirds

$^1/_2$ cup jellied cranberry sauce

2 tablespoons honey mustard dressing

$^1/_2$ teaspoon ground mustard

1 to 2 tablespoons chopped fresh chives

1 In shallow bowl, mix turkey and $^1/_2$ cup honey mustard dressing. Cover and refrigerate 30 minutes to marinate.

2 Remove turkey from marinade; discard marinade. Wrap bacon piece around each turkey piece; secure with toothpick. Place on ungreased broiler pan rack.

3 Broil with tops 4 to 6 inches from heat 8 to 12 minutes, turning once, until turkey is no longer pink in center and bacon begins to look crisp.

4 Meanwhile, in 1-quart saucepan, mix cranberry sauce, 2 tablespoons honey mustard dressing and mustard. Cook over low heat, stirring occasionally, just until melted and well blended; cool slightly. Just before serving, sprinkle with chives. Serve turkey bites with sauce.

Do Ahead: Prepare and bake these turkey bites up to 24 hours in advance. Cover tightly and refrigerate. Just before serving, heat at 375°F about 15 minutes or until hot.

1 Appetizer: Calories 50 (Calories from Fat 25); Total Fat 3g (Saturated Fat 1g); Cholesterol 10mg; Sodium 80mg; Total Carbohydrate 3g (Dietary Fiber 0g); Protein 3g

2

satisfying salads

italian chopped salad

Prep Time: 20 min ▪ **Start to Finish:** 20 min ▪ 4 Servings

6 cups chopped romaine lettuce

1 cup fresh basil leaves

1 cup cut-up deli rotisserie or other cooked chicken (about 8 oz)

2 large tomatoes, chopped (2 cups)

2 medium cucumbers, chopped (1¹/₂ cups)

3 oz Italian salami, chopped

1 can (15 oz) cannellini beans, drained, rinsed

²/₃ cup red wine vinaigrette or Italian dressing

1 In large bowl, place all ingredients except dressing.

2 Pour dressing over salad; toss until coated.

1 Serving: Calories 500 (Calories from Fat 240); Total Fat 27g (Saturated Fat 4.5g); Cholesterol 55mg; Sodium 940mg; Total Carbohydrate 36g (Dietary Fiber 10g); Protein 27g

grilled chicken citrus salad

Prep Time: 30 min ▪ **Start to Finish:** 30 min ▪ 4 Servings

$^2/_3$ cup citrus vinaigrette dressing
4 boneless skinless chicken breasts (about 1$^1/_4$ lb)
1 bag (10 oz) ready-to-eat romaine lettuce
2 unpeeled apples, cubed (about 2 cups)
$^1/_2$ cup coarsely chopped dried apricots
2 medium green onions, sliced (2 tablespoons)
$^1/_2$ cup chopped honey-roasted peanuts

1 Heat gas or charcoal grill. In small bowl, place 2 tablespoons of the dressing. Brush all sides of chicken with the 2 tablespoons dressing.

2 In large bowl, toss lettuce, apples, apricots and onions; set aside.

3 Place chicken on grill. Cover grill; cook over medium heat 8 to 10 minutes, turning once, until juice of chicken is clear when center of thickest part is cut (170°F).

4 Add remaining dressing to lettuce mixture; toss. On 4 plates, divide lettuce mixture. Cut chicken crosswise into slices; place on lettuce. Sprinkle with peanuts.

1 Serving: Calories 550 (Calories from Fat 280); Total Fat 31g (Saturated Fat 4g); Cholesterol 90mg; Sodium 510mg; Total Carbohydrate 30g (Dietary Fiber 6g); Protein 39g

There are so many enticing prewashed salad greens available—feel free to use your favorite for this recipe.

southwestern chicken blt salad

Prep Time: 20 min ▪ **Start to Finish:** 20 min ▪ 6 Servings

Salsa-Bacon Dressing

$\frac{1}{2}$ cup chunky-style salsa

$\frac{1}{2}$ cup nonfat ranch dressing

1 tablespoon chopped fresh parsley

Salad

1 bag (10 oz) romaine and leaf lettuce mix

2 packages (6 oz each) refrigerated cooked
    Southwest-flavor chicken breast strips

4 plum (Roma) tomatoes, coarsely chopped

$\frac{1}{2}$ cup chopped cooked bacon

$\frac{1}{2}$ cup croutons

1 In small bowl, mix dressing ingredients; set aside.

2 In large bowl, mix salad ingredients. Add dressing; toss until coated.

1 Serving: Calories 190 (Calories from Fat 60); Total Fat 7g (Saturated Fat 2g); Cholesterol 55mg; Sodium 530mg; Total Carbohydrate 12g (Dietary Fiber 2g); Protein 21g

Save some chopping time. Use 1 cup cherry tomatoes, cut in half, instead of the plum tomatoes.

mandarin chicken salad

Prep Time: 20 min ▪ **Start to Finish:** 20 min ▪ 6 Servings

2 tablespoons butter or margarine

1 package (3 oz) Oriental-flavor ramen noodle soup mix

2 tablespoons sesame seed

$^1/_4$ cup sugar

$^1/_4$ cup white vinegar

1 tablespoon sesame or vegetable oil

$^1/_2$ teaspoon pepper

2 cups cut-up cooked chicken (about 1 lb)

$^1/_4$ cup dry-roasted peanuts, if desired

4 medium green onions, sliced ($^1/_4$ cup)

1 bag (10 oz) European-style or romaine lettuce

1 can (11 oz) mandarin orange segments, drained

1 In 10-inch skillet, melt butter over medium heat. Stir in seasoning packet from soup mix. Break block of noodles into bite-size pieces over skillet; stir into butter mixture.

2 Cook noodles 2 minutes, stirring occasionally. Stir in sesame seed. Cook about 2 minutes longer, stirring occasionally, until noodles are golden brown; remove from heat.

3 In large bowl, mix sugar, vinegar, oil and pepper. Add noodle mixture and remaining ingredients; toss.

1 Serving: Calories 300 (Calories from Fat 130); Total Fat 14g (Saturated Fat 4.5g); Cholesterol 50mg; Sodium 330mg; Total Carbohydrate 28g (Dietary Fiber 4g); Protein 17g

grilled chicken satay salad

Prep Time: 35 min ■ **Start to Finish:** 1 hr 35 min ■ 6 Servings

Salad

1 flour tortilla (8 inch), cut in half, then cut
    crosswise into $1/8$- to $1/4$-inch strips
4 boneless, skinless chicken breasts (about $1^1/4$ lb)
6 cups bite-size pieces mixed salad greens
1 cup finely shredded red cabbage
$1/3$ cup julienne (matchstick-cut) carrot
$1/4$ cup chopped fresh cilantro or parsley

Peanut Satay Dressing*

$1/3$ cup rice vinegar or cider vinegar
$1/4$ cup creamy peanut butter
3 tablespoons finely chopped peanuts
2 tablespoons sugar
2 tablespoons vegetable oil
2 tablespoons sesame oil
1 tablespoon soy sauce
$1/2$ teaspoon finely chopped gingerroot
1 clove garlic, finely chopped

1 Heat oven to 350°F. On ungreased cookie sheet, arrange tortilla strips in single layer. Bake 7 to 11 minutes or until lightly browned.

2 Meanwhile, in small bowl, beat all dressing ingredients with whisk until smooth and creamy. Place chicken in resealable food-storage plastic bag; add 3 tablespoons of the dressing. Seal bag; turn to coat chicken. Refrigerate 1 to 2 hours. Refrigerate remaining dressing. In large bowl, toss remaining ingredients; cover and refrigerate.

3 Brush grill rack with vegetable oil. Heat gas or charcoal grill for direct heat. Cover and grill chicken 4 to 6 inches from medium heat 10 to 15 minutes, turning once, until juice of chicken is clear when center of thickest part is cut to bone.

4 Cut chicken into strips. Add chicken and remaining dressing to salad; toss. Divide salad among 6 plates. Sprinkle with tortilla strips.

*About $3/4$ cup purchased peanut dressing can be substituted for the Peanut Satay Dressing.

1 Serving: Calories 335 (Calories from Fat 180); Total Fat 20g (Saturated Fat 4g); Cholesterol 50mg; Sodium 320mg; Total Carbohydrate 15g (Dietary Fiber 3g); Protein 24g

asian chicken salad lettuce cups

Prep Time: 15 min ▐ **Start to Finish:** 15 min ▐ 24 Appetizers

2 cups finely chopped cooked chicken (about 1 lb)

4 medium green onions, diagonally sliced (¼ cup)

1 can (8 oz) sliced water chestnuts, drained, finely chopped

½ cup spicy peanut sauce (from 7-oz bottle)

1 tablespoon chopped fresh mint leaves

¼ teaspoon crushed red pepper flakes

24 small (about 3-inch) Bibb lettuce leaves (about 1½ heads), breaking larger leaves into smaller size

½ cup chopped roasted salted peanuts

1 In medium bowl, mix all ingredients except lettuce and peanuts.

2 Spoon about 2 tablespoons chicken mixture onto each lettuce leaf. Sprinkle with peanuts.

1 Appetizer: Calories 60 (Calories from Fat 35); Total Fat 3.5g (Saturated Fat 0.5g); Cholesterol 10mg; Sodium 35mg; Total Carbohydrate 2g (Dietary Fiber 0g); Protein 5g

Wrap and roll! This cute finger food is fresh and crunchy—it's also perfect for your pals who are avoiding bread.

pasta-chicken salad on watermelon wedges

Prep Time: 15 min ■ **Start to Finish:** 15 min ■ 6 Servings

1½ cups uncooked mini penne pasta or other small pasta (about 6 oz)

2 cups cut-up cooked chicken breast (about 1 lb)

1 cup red grapes, cut in half

8 medium green onions, sliced (½ cup)

¾ cup reduced-calorie mayonnaise or salad dressing

3 tablespoons fat-free (skim) milk

1 tablespoon Dijon mustard

½ teaspoon salt

18 watermelon wedges, 1 inch thick

¼ cup sliced almonds, toasted

1 Cook and drain pasta as directed on package. Rinse with cold water; drain.

2 In large bowl, mix pasta, chicken, grapes and onions. In small bowl, mix mayonnaise, milk, mustard and salt; stir into pasta mixture.

3 To serve, place 3 watermelon wedges on each of 6 dinner plates. Divide salad evenly among watermelon wedges. Sprinkle with almonds.

1 Serving: Calories 520 (Calories from Fat 150); Total Fat 17g (Saturated Fat 2.5g); Cholesterol 50mg; Sodium 620mg; Total Carbohydrate 72g (Dietary Fiber 5g); Protein 23g

wild rice–chicken salad

Prep Time: 15 min ■ **Start to Finish:** 15 min ■ 4 Servings

Basil Vinaigrette

$^1/_4$ cup olive or vegetable oil

3 tablespoons raspberry vinegar or red wine vinegar

1 tablespoon chopped fresh basil leaves

$^1/_4$ teaspoon salt

$^1/_4$ teaspoon pepper

Salad

1 pint (2 cups) deli chicken salad

1 can (15 oz) cooked wild rice, drained

$^1/_2$ cup dried cranberries

Boston lettuce leaves

1 In small bowl, mix vinaigrette ingredients.

2 In large bowl, mix salad ingredients except lettuce. Toss with vinaigrette until coated. Serve on lettuce.

1 Serving: Calories 475 (Calories from Fat 235); Total Fat 26g (Saturated Fat 4g); Cholesterol 45mg; Sodium 380mg; Total Carbohydrate 42g (Dietary Fiber 4g); Protein 18g

grilled steak and potato salad

Prep Time: 30 min ■ **Start to Finish:** 30 min ■ 4 Servings

$3/4$ **lb small red potatoes, cut in half**

$2/3$ **cup honey Dijon dressing**

1 boneless beef top sirloin or round steak, $3/4$ inch thick ($3/4$ lb)

$1/4$ **teaspoon salt**

$1/4$ **teaspoon coarsely ground pepper**

4 cups bite-size pieces romaine lettuce

2 medium tomatoes, cut into thin wedges

$1/2$ **cup thinly sliced red onion**

Additional pepper, if desired

1 Heat gas or charcoal grill. In 2- or $2^{1}/_{2}$-quart saucepan, place potatoes; add enough water to cover potatoes. Heat to boiling; reduce heat to medium. Cook uncovered 5 to 8 minutes or just until potatoes are tender.

2 Drain potatoes; place in medium bowl. Add 2 tablespoons of the dressing; toss to coat. Place potatoes in grill basket (grill "wok") if desired. Brush beef steak with 1 tablespoon of the dressing; sprinkle with salt and pepper.

3 Place beef and potatoes on grill. Cover grill; cook over medium heat 8 to 15 minutes, turning once, until beef is desired doneness and potatoes are golden brown. Cut beef into thin slices.

4 Among 4 plates, divide lettuce, tomatoes and onion. Top with beef and potatoes; drizzle with remaining dressing. Sprinkle with additional pepper.

1 Serving: Calories 360 (Calories from Fat 180); Total Fat 20g (Saturated Fat 4g); Cholesterol 35mg; Sodium 440mg; Total Carbohydrate 25g (Dietary Fiber 4g); Protein 22g

Try adding a generous sprinkle of crumbled blue or Gorgonzola cheese to top these salads.

fajita salad

Prep Time: 20 min ▪ **Start to Finish:** 20 min ▪ 4 Servings

$^3/_4$ lb lean beef boneless sirloin steak

1 tablespoon vegetable oil

2 medium bell peppers, cut into strips

1 small onion, thinly sliced

4 cups bite-size pieces salad greens

$^1/_3$ cup Italian dressing

$^1/_4$ cup plain yogurt

1 Cut beef with grain into 2-inch strips; cut strips across grain into $^1/_8$-inch slices.

2 In 10-inch nonstick skillet, heat oil over medium-high heat. Cook beef in oil about 3 minutes, stirring occasionally, until brown. Remove beef from skillet.

3 In same skillet, cook bell peppers and onion about 3 minutes, stirring occasionally, until bell peppers are crisp-tender. Stir in beef.

4 Place salad greens on serving platter. Top with beef mixture. In small bowl, mix dressing and yogurt; drizzle over salad.

1 Serving: Calories 255 (Calories from Fat 135); Total Fat 15g (Saturated Fat 2g); Cholesterol 50mg; Sodium 240mg; Total Carbohydrate 10g (Dietary Fiber 3g); Protein 20g

Check out the meat case for precut meats. In addition to being a time-saver, these precut meats often come in small, one-time-use portions, which increases your options.

fiesta taco salad with beans

Prep Time: 20 min ▪ **Start to Finish:** 20 min ▪ 5 Servings

1 can (15 oz) black beans, rinsed, drained
$^1/_2$ cup taco sauce
6 cups lettuce, torn into bite-size pieces
1 medium green bell pepper, cut into strips
2 medium tomatoes, cut into wedges
$^1/_2$ cup pitted ripe olives, drained
1 cup corn chips
1 cup shredded Cheddar cheese (4 oz)
$^1/_2$ cup reduced-fat Thousand Island dressing

1 In 2-quart saucepan, cook beans and taco sauce over medium heat 4 to 5 minutes, stirring occasionally, until thoroughly heated.

2 In large bowl, toss lettuce, bell pepper, tomatoes, olives and corn chips. Spoon bean mixture over lettuce mixture; toss. Sprinkle with cheese. Serve immediately with dressing.

1 Serving (2 cups): Calories 350 (Calories from Fat 130); Total Fat 15g (Saturated Fat 6g); Cholesterol 25mg; Sodium 980mg; Total Carbohydrate 40g (Dietary Fiber 8g); Protein 15g

Cut back on the fat and calories by using reduced-fat Cheddar cheese and fat-free Thousand Island dressing.

mediterranean quinoa salad

Prep Time: 30 min ■ **Start to Finish:** 1 hr 35 min ■ 4 Servings

1 cup uncooked quinoa

2 cups roasted garlic–seasoned chicken broth (from two 14-oz cans)

$^1/_2$ cup chopped drained roasted red bell peppers (from 7-oz jar)

$^1/_2$ cup cubed provolone cheese

$^1/_4$ cup chopped kalamata olives

2 tablespoons chopped fresh basil leaves

2 tablespoons fat-free Italian dressing

1 Rinse quinoa under cold water 1 minute; drain.

2 In 2-quart saucepan, heat quinoa and broth to boiling; reduce heat. Cover and simmer 15 to 20 minutes or until quinoa is tender; drain. Cool completely, about 45 minutes.

3 In large serving bowl, toss quinoa and remaining ingredients. Serve immediately, or refrigerate 1 to 2 hours before serving.

1 Serving: Calories 260 (Calories from Fat 80); Total Fat 9g (Saturated Fat 3.5g); Cholesterol 10mg; Sodium 820mg; Total Carbohydrate 33g (Dietary Fiber 3g); Protein 13g

Quinoa is a popular grain in South American cuisine and is gaining popularity in the United States.

picnic pasta salad

Prep Time: 20 min ■ **Start to Finish:** 2 hr 20 min ■ 26 Servings

1 package (16 oz) bow-tie (farfalle) pasta
1 can (8 oz) tomato sauce
1 cup Italian dressing
1 tablespoon chopped fresh or 1 teaspoon dried basil leaves
1 tablespoon chopped fresh or 1 teaspoon dried oregano leaves
1 cup sliced fresh mushrooms (3 oz)
5 plum (Roma) tomatoes, coarsely chopped (1¹/₂ cups)
1 large cucumber, coarsely chopped (1¹/₂ cups)
1 medium red onion, chopped (1¹/₂ cups)
1 can (2.25 oz) sliced ripe olives, drained

1 Cook and drain pasta as directed on package. Rinse with cold water; drain.

2 In large bowl, mix tomato sauce, dressing, basil and oregano. Add pasta and remaining ingredients; toss. Cover and refrigerate at least 2 hours until chilled but no longer than 48 hours.

1 Serving (¹/₂ cup): Calories 120 (Calories from Fat 40); Total Fat 4.5g (Saturated Fat 0g); Cholesterol 0mg; Sodium 220mg; Total Carbohydrate 17g (Dietary Fiber 2g); Protein 3g

Don't like mushrooms? Go ahead and use roasted red bell pepper slices instead.

mediterranean potato salad

Prep Time: 25 min ▪ **Start to Finish:** 25 min ▪ 12 Servings

1¹/₂ lb medium red potatoes, cut in half
3 slices bacon
³/₄ cup red or yellow grape tomatoes
³/₄ cup chopped onion
³/₄ cup sliced ripe olives
¹/₂ cup fat-free Italian dressing
1 tablespoon cider vinegar
1 tablespoon chopped fresh Italian parsley, if desired

1 In 3-quart saucepan, heat 1 inch water to boiling. Add potatoes. Cover and heat to boiling; reduce heat. Cover and simmer 10 to 15 minutes or until tender; drain. Cool slightly. Cut potatoes into ³/₄-inch cubes; place in large bowl.

2 Meanwhile, line microwavable plate with microwavable paper towel. Place bacon on paper towel; top with another microwavable paper towel. Microwave on High 2 to 3 minutes or until bacon is crisp. Crumble bacon.

3 Stir bacon, tomatoes, onion and olives into warm cubed potatoes. In small bowl, mix dressing and vinegar; pour over potato mixture, stirring gently to coat vegetables. Sprinkle with parsley. Serve warm or cool.

1 Serving (¹/₂ cup): Calories 60 (Calories from Fat 15): Total Fat 1.5g (Saturated Fat 0g); Cholesterol 0mg; Sodium 170mg; Total Carbohydrate 12g (Dietary Fiber 2g); Protein 2g

Serve this delicious side with grilled turkey or chicken sausage for an easy summer meal!

3

sandwiches and pizza

chicken salad roll-ups

Prep Time: 35 min ■ **Start to Finish:** 1 hr 35 min ■ 24 Roll-Ups

2 cups chopped cooked chicken
3 medium green onions, chopped (3 tablespoons)
¹/₄ cup chopped walnuts
¹/₂ cup creamy poppy seed dressing
¹/₂ cup cream cheese spread (from 8-oz container)
2 flour tortillas (10 inch)
6 leaves Bibb lettuce
¹/₂ cup finely chopped strawberries

1 In food processor bowl, mix chicken, onions and walnuts. Cover and process by using quick on-and-off motions until finely chopped. Add ¹/₃ cup of the poppy seed dressing; process only until mixed. In small bowl, mix remaining dressing and the cream cheese with spoon until smooth.

2 Spread cream cheese mixture evenly over entire surface of tortillas. Remove white rib from lettuce leaves. Press lettuce into cream cheese, tearing to fit and leaving top 2 inches of tortillas uncovered. Spread chicken mixture over lettuce. Sprinkle strawberries over chicken.

3 Firmly roll up tortillas, beginning at bottom. Wrap each roll in plastic wrap. Refrigerate at least 1 hour. Trim ends of each roll. Cut rolls into ¹/₂- to ³/₄-inch slices.

1 Roll-Up: Calories 70 (Calories from Fat 35); Total Fat 4g (Saturated Fat 1.5g); Cholesterol 20mg; Sodium 50mg; Total Carbohydrate 5g (Dietary Fiber 0g); Protein 4g

If transporting this appetizer, place the roll-ups in a covered container in an insulated cooler with plenty of ice packs to keep them cold until ready to serve.

cranberry–chicken salad puffs

Prep Time: 25 min ▪ **Start to Finish:** 1 hr ▪ 20 Puffs

$^{1}/_{2}$ **cup water**
$^{1}/_{4}$ **cup butter or margarine**
$^{1}/_{2}$ **cup all-purpose flour**
2 eggs
$^{1}/_{2}$ **pint chicken salad (1 cup; from deli)**
$^{1}/_{4}$ **cup dried cranberries**
$^{1}/_{4}$ **cup chopped pistachio nuts**
1 teaspoon chopped fresh or $^{1}/_{4}$ teaspoon dried marjoram leaves

1 Heat oven to 400°F. Grease cookie sheet with shortening or spray with cooking spray. In $2^{1}/_{2}$-quart saucepan, heat water and butter to rolling boil. Stir in flour; reduce heat to low. Stir vigorously over low heat about 1 minute or until mixture forms a ball; remove from heat.

2 Beat in eggs all at once with spoon; continue beating until smooth. Drop dough by heaping teaspoonfuls about 2 inches apart onto cookie sheet.

3 Bake about 18 minutes or until puffed and golden brown. Remove from oven; cut small slit with knife in side of each puff to allow steam to escape. Return to oven; bake 2 minutes longer. Cool away from draft about 10 minutes.

4 Meanwhile, in medium bowl, mix chicken salad, cranberries, nuts and marjoram.

5 Cut off top third of each puff; pull out any strands of dough. Spoon heaping teaspoonful of chicken salad into each puff.

Do Ahead: Assemble these appetizers and refrigerate up to 2 hours before serving. Relax and enjoy the party!

1 Puff: Calories 75 (Calories from Fat 45); Total Fat 5g (Saturated Fat 2g); Cholesterol 30mg; Sodium 50mg; Total Carbohydrate 5g (Dietary Fiber 0g); Protein 3g

beef and provolone pinwheels

Prep Time: 10 min ▪ **Start to Finish:** 10 min ▪ 24 Pinwheels

$\frac{1}{4}$ **cup mayonnaise or salad dressing**

2 cloves garlic, finely chopped

2 flour tortillas (8 inch; from 11.5-oz package)

1 cup fresh spinach

$\frac{1}{4}$ **lb thinly sliced roast beef (from deli)**

6 slices ($\frac{3}{4}$ oz each) provolone cheese

1 medium tomato, thinly sliced

24 toothpicks

1 In small bowl, mix mayonnaise and garlic. Spread mixture evenly over tortillas.

2 Top tortillas with layers of spinach, beef, cheese and tomato; roll up tightly. Cut each tortilla into 12 pieces; secure with toothpicks. Serve immediately, or refrigerate until serving.

Do Ahead: Wrap each uncut roll tightly in plastic wrap and refrigerate up to 24 hours.

1 Pinwheel: Calories 55 (Calories from Fat 35); Total Fat 4g (Saturated Fat 2g); Cholesterol 10mg; Sodium 85mg; Total Carbohydrate 2g (Dietary Fiber 0g); Protein 3g

curried egg salad sandwiches

Prep Time: 15 min ■ **Start to Finish:** 15 min ■ 2 Sandwiches

3 hard-cooked eggs, chopped

$1/4$ cup fat-free mayonnaise or salad dressing

$1/4$ teaspoon salt

$1/4$ teaspoon curry powder

$1/4$ cup shredded carrot

2 tablespoons finely chopped onion

2 tablespoons coarsely chopped cashews

4 slices whole-grain bread

1 In small bowl, stir together all ingredients except bread.

2 Spread egg mixture on 2 slices bread. Top with remaining bread.

1 Sandwich: Calories 340 (Calories from Fat 140); Total Fat 15g (Saturated Fat 4g); Cholesterol 320mg; Sodium 960mg; Total Carbohydrate 36g (Dietary Fiber 5g); Protein 17g

Prepare these perfectly portable sandwiches in advance. Make the egg salad the night before, and assemble the sandwiches in the morning. Add an ice pack to your lunch box or picnic basket, and you're ready to go.

mushroom-pepper whole wheat sandwiches

Prep Time: 30 min ■ **Start to Finish:** 30 min ■ 4 Sandwiches

4 medium fresh portabella mushroom caps (3½ to 4 inch)

4 slices red onion, ½ inch thick

2 tablespoons reduced-fat mayonnaise or salad dressing

2 teaspoons reduced-fat balsamic vinaigrette

8 slices whole wheat bread

4 slices (¾ oz each) reduced-fat mozzarella cheese

8 strips (2×1 inch) roasted red bell pepper (from 7-oz jar), patted dry

8 large basil leaves

1 Heat closed medium-size contact grill for 5 minutes.

2 Place mushrooms on grill. Close grill; cook 4 to 5 minutes or until slightly softened. Remove mushrooms from grill. Place onion on grill. Close grill; cook 4 to 5 minutes or until slightly softened. Remove onion from grill.

3 In small bowl, mix mayonnaise and vinaigrette; spread over bread slices. Top 4 bread slices with mushrooms, cheese, onion, bell pepper and basil. Top with remaining bread, mayonnaise sides down.

4 Place 2 sandwiches on grill. Close grill; cook 2 to 3 minutes or until sandwiches are golden brown and toasted. Repeat with remaining 2 sandwiches.

1 Sandwich: Calories 260 (Calories from Fat 80); Total Fat 9g (Saturated Fat 3g); Cholesterol 10mg; Sodium 440mg; Total Carbohydrate 32g (Dietary Fiber 5g); Protein 14g

onion and bacon grilled cheese sandwiches

Prep Time: 25 min ■ **Start to Finish:** 25 min ■ 4 Sandwiches

4 slices bacon, cut into $1/2$-inch pieces
1 medium onion, thinly sliced
8 slices (1 oz each) Cheddar cheese
8 slices Vienna bread, $1/2$ inch thick

1 In 12-inch nonstick skillet, cook bacon over medium heat about 4 minutes, stirring occasionally, until almost cooked.

2 Add onion to skillet. Cook 2 to 3 minutes, turning occasionally, until tender. Remove bacon and onion from skillet. Reserve 1 tablespoon drippings in skillet.

3 To make each sandwich, layer cheese, bacon and onion between 2 bread slices. Place 2 sandwiches in drippings in skillet. Cover; cook over medium-low heat 3 to 5 minutes, turning once, until bread is crisp and golden brown and cheese is melted. Repeat with remaining 2 sandwiches.

1 Sandwich: Calories 350 (Calories from Fat 170); Total Fat 19g (Saturated Fat 10g); Cholesterol 55mg; Sodium 730mg; Total Carbohydrate 27g (Dietary Fiber 2g); Protein 18g

The Vienna bread is great here, but feel free to use whatever bread you like best.

caesar chicken paninis

Prep Time: 30 min ◾ **Start to Finish:** 30 min ◾ 4 Sandwiches

4 boneless skinless chicken breasts (about 1^1/$_4$ lb)
4 hard rolls (about 5×3 inches), split
4 slices red onion
1 large tomato, sliced
^{1}/$_3$ cup Caesar dressing
^{1}/$_4$ cup shredded Parmesan cheese (1 oz)
4 leaves romaine lettuce

1 Flatten each chicken breast to ^{1}/$_4$-inch thickness with meat mallet or rolling pin between sheets of plastic wrap or waxed paper.

2 Spray 8- or 10-inch skillet with cooking spray; heat over medium-high heat. Cook chicken in skillet 10 to 15 minutes, turning once, until chicken is no longer pink in center. Remove chicken from skillet; keep warm.

3 In skillet, place rolls, cut sides down. Cook over medium heat about 2 minutes or until toasted. Place lettuce on bottom halves of rolls. Top with chicken, dressing, onion, tomato, cheese, and tops of rolls.

1 Sandwich: Calories 500 (Calories from Fat 180); Total Fat 20g (Saturated Fat 4.5g); Cholesterol 90mg; Sodium 750mg; Total Carbohydrate 37g (Dietary Fiber 3g); Protein 41g

Keep it easy and serve with raw baby carrots and red and green grapes.

grilled chicken-cheddar sandwiches

Prep Time: 35 min ■ **Start to Finish:** 35 min ■ 4 Sandwiches

4 boneless skinless chicken breasts (about $1^1/_4$ lb)

$^1/_2$ teaspoon seasoned salt

$^1/_4$ teaspoon coarse pepper

1 medium Bermuda or other sweet onion, sliced

4 oz fresh mushrooms, cut in half ($1^1/_2$ cups)

1 tablespoon olive or vegetable oil

3 tablespoons creamy Dijon mustard-mayonnaise spread

4 slices ($^2/_3$ oz each) sharp Cheddar cheese

4 slices sourdough bread

1 Heat gas or charcoal grill for direct heat. Flatten each chicken breast to $^1/_4$-inch thickness between sheets of plastic wrap or waxed paper. Sprinkle with $^1/_4$ teaspoon of the seasoned salt and the pepper.

2 In medium bowl, mix onion, mushrooms, remaining $^1/_4$ teaspoon seasoned salt and the oil; toss to coat. Place in grill basket. Place chicken on grill next to grill basket. Cover and grill chicken and vegetables 4 to 6 inches from medium heat 10 to 15 minutes, occasionally turning and brushing chicken with 2 tablespoons of the mustard-mayonnaise spread and shaking grill basket to mix vegetables. Grill until chicken is no longer pink in center and vegetables are tender. Add bread slices to grill for last 4 minutes of cooking, turning once, until crisp.

3 Top each cooked chicken breast with onion-mushroom mixture and cheese slice. Cover grill until cheese is melted. Spread bread slices with remaining mustard-mayonnaise spread. Top each bread slice with cheese-topped chicken breast.

1 Sandwich: Calories 380 (Calories from Fat 160); Total Fat 18g (Saturated Fat 7g); Cholesterol 100mg; Sodium 590mg; Total Carbohydrate 19g (Dietary Fiber 2g); Protein 35g

Mix it up. Try using Swiss or Monterey Jack cheese instead of the sharp Cheddar.

chicken blt sandwiches

Prep Time: 30 min ▪ **Start to Finish:** 30 min ▪ 4 Sandwiches

4 boneless skinless chicken breasts (about 1¼ lb)
¼ cup Thousand Island dressing
4 whole wheat sandwich buns, split
4 lettuce leaves
8 slices tomato
4 slices bacon, cooked, drained and broken in half

1 Heat gas or charcoal grill for direct heat. Cover and grill chicken 4 to 6 inches from medium heat 15 to 20 minutes, turning once or twice, until juice of chicken is clear when center of thickest part is cut.

2 Spread dressing on cut sides of buns. Layer lettuce, chicken, tomato and bacon on bottoms of buns. Top with tops of buns.

1 Sandwich: Calories 320 (Calories from Fat 125); Total Fat 14g (Saturated Fat 3g); Cholesterol 80mg; Sodium 450mg; Total Carbohydrate 20g (Dietary Fiber 3g); Protein 32g

Save some time! Look for already-cooked bacon. It's in the supermarket with the regular bacon. All you have to do is reheat it in the microwave.

prosciutto-pesto napoleons

Prep Time: 25 min ∎ **Start to Finish:** 1 hr 25 min ∎ 24 Napoleons

1 sheet frozen puff pastry (from 17.3-oz box)

1 egg, beaten

1 tablespoon sesame seed

¹/₄ cup refrigerated basil pesto (from 7-oz container)

1 cup roasted red bell peppers (from 7-oz jar), cut into thin strips and drained on paper towels

¹/₄ lb thinly sliced prosciutto, cut crosswise into strips

1 Thaw pastry at room temperature 30 minutes. Heat oven to 400°F. Unfold pastry; brush top with egg. Sprinkle with sesame seed. Cut pastry into thirds along fold lines. Cut each strip crosswise into eight 3×1¹/₄-inches rectangles. On ungreased cookie sheets, place rectangles 2 inches apart.

2 Bake about 15 minutes or until puffed and golden brown. Remove from cookie sheets to cooling rack. Cool completely, about 15 minutes.

3 Cut each rectangle in half horizontally. Spread ¹/₂ teaspoon pesto on cut side of bottom of each rectangle. Top with bell peppers and prosciutto strips. Place tops of rectangles over prosciutto.

1 Napoleon: Calories 80 (Calories from Fat 50); Total Fat 5g (Saturated Fat 1.5g); Cholesterol 20mg; Sodium 105mg; Total Carbohydrate 5g (Dietary Fiber 0g); Protein 2g

cajun pork burgers

Prep Time: 20 min ▪ **Start to Finish:** 25 min ▪ 4 Sandwiches

1 tablespoon olive or vegetable oil

1$^1/_2$ cups frozen bell pepper and onion stir-fry (from 1-lb bag)

1 medium stalk celery, sliced ($^1/_2$ cup)

2 tablespoons chopped fresh parsley

1 lb ground pork

2 tablespoons chili sauce

$^1/_2$ teaspoon garlic salt

$^1/_4$ teaspoon dried thyme leaves

$^1/_8$ teaspoon ground red pepper (cayenne)

4 sandwich buns

1 Heat oven to 375°F. In 10-inch nonstick skillet, heat oil over medium-high heat. Cook frozen bell pepper mixture and celery in oil 3 to 4 minutes, stirring occasionally, until tender. Stir in parsley; remove mixture from skillet. Cover to keep warm.

2 In large bowl, mix pork, chili sauce, garlic salt, thyme and red pepper. Shape mixture into 4 oval patties, $^1/_2$ inch thick. Cook patties in hot skillet over medium heat 8 to 10 minutes, turning once, until no longer pink in center.

3 Place buns, cut sides up, on ungreased cookie sheet. Bake 3 to 5 minutes or until toasted. Serve patties topped with vegetables on buns.

1 Sandwich: Calories 370 (Calories from Fat 190); Total Fat 21g (Saturated Fat 7g); Cholesterol 70mg; Sodium 470mg; Total Carbohydrate 24g (Dietary Fiber 2g); Protein 24g

spiced pork tenderloin crostini

Prep Time: 30 min ■ **Start to Finish:** 1 hr 10 min ■ 36 Crostini

$^1/_2$ **teaspoon seasoned salt**

$^1/_2$ **teaspoon garlic pepper**

$^1/_2$ **teaspoon dried marjoram leaves**

$^1/_4$ **teaspoon ground sage**

1 lb pork tenderloin

36 slices ($^1/_4$- to $^1/_2$-inch thick) baguette-style French bread (from 10-oz loaf)

$^1/_4$ **cup Dijon mustard**

$^3/_4$ **cup apple-cranberry chutney (from 8.5-oz jar)**

$^1/_3$ **cup crumbled blue cheese**

Fresh marjoram leaves

1 Heat oven to 425°F. In small bowl, mix seasoned salt, garlic pepper, marjoram and sage. Rub mixture over pork. Place pork in shallow roasting pan. Insert meat thermometer so tip is in thickest part of pork. Bake uncovered 20 to 25 minutes or until thermometer reads 155°F. Cover pork with foil and let stand 10 to 15 minutes or until thermometer reads 160°F.

2 Meanwhile, reduce oven temperature to 375°F. Place bread slices in ungreased 15×10×1-inch pan. Bake about 5 minutes or until crisp; cool.

3 Cut pork into very thin slices. Spread each bread slice with about $^1/_4$ teaspoon mustard. Top each with a thin slice of pork, 1 teaspoon chutney, about $^1/_2$ teaspoon cheese and the marjoram leaves.

1 Crostini: Calories 55 (Calories from Fat 10); Total Fat 1g (Saturated Fat 0g); Cholesterol 10mg; Sodium 140mg; Total Carbohydrate 7g (Dietary Fiber 0g); Protein 4g

chewy pizza bread

Prep Time: 10 min ■ **Start to Finish:** 30 min ■ 4 Servings

1¹/₂ cups all-purpose flour
1¹/₂ teaspoons baking powder
¹/₂ teaspoon salt
³/₄ cup regular or nonalcoholic beer
¹/₂ cup tomato pasta sauce
¹/₃ cup shredded mozzarella cheese (1.5 oz)
Chopped fresh basil leaves, if desired

1 Heat oven to 425°F. Spray 8-inch square pan with cooking spray.

2 In medium bowl, mix flour, baking powder and salt. Stir in beer just until flour is moistened. Spread dough in pan. Spread pasta sauce over dough. Sprinkle with cheese.

3 Bake 15 to 20 minutes or until toothpick inserted in center comes out clean. Sprinkle with basil. Cut into 2-inch squares. Serve warm.

1 Serving (4 squares): Calories 230 (Calories from Fat 30); Total Fat 3.5g (Saturated Fat 1.5g); Cholesterol 5mg; Sodium 680mg; Total Carbohydrate 43g (Dietary Fiber 2g); Protein 8g

double-cheese, spinach and chicken pizza

Prep Time: 5 min ▪ **Start to Finish:** 15 min ▪ 6 Servings

1 package (14 oz) prebaked original Italian pizza crust (12 inch)

1 cup shredded Havarti cheese (4 oz)

2 cups washed fresh baby spinach leaves (from 10-oz bag)

1 cup diced deli rotisserie or other cooked chicken (about 8 oz)

$^1/_4$ cup chopped drained roasted red bell peppers (from 7-oz jar)

$^1/_2$ teaspoon garlic salt

1 cup shredded Cheddar cheese (4 oz)

1 Heat oven to 425°F. Place pizza crust on ungreased cookie sheet.

2 Top with Havarti cheese, spinach, chicken, bell peppers, garlic salt and Cheddar cheese.

3 Bake 8 to 10 minutes or until crust is golden brown.

1 Serving: Calories 380 (Calories from Fat 170); Total Fat 19g (Saturated Fat 11g); Cholesterol 70mg; Sodium 800mg; Total Carbohydrate 30g (Dietary Fiber 2g); Protein 23g

chicken gyro pizza

Prep Time: 20 min ▪ **Start to Finish:** 45 min ▪ 6 Servings

2 cups Original Bisquick mix
$^1/_4$ teaspoon dried oregano leaves
$^1/_2$ cup cold water
6 slices chicken breast, cut into strips
1 can (2$^1/_4$ oz) sliced ripe olives, drained
$^1/_2$ cup crumbled feta cheese (2 oz)
1$^1/_2$ cups shredded mozzarella cheese (6 oz)
1 small tomato, chopped ($^1/_2$ cup)
$^1/_2$ cup chopped cucumber

1 Move oven rack to lowest position. Heat oven to 425°F. Spray 12-inch pizza pan with cooking spray. In medium bowl, stir Bisquick mix, oregano and water; beat vigorously with spoon 20 strokes until soft dough forms. Press dough in pizza pan, using fingers dipped in Bisquick mix; pinch edge to form $^1/_2$-inch rim. Bake about 15 minutes or until golden brown.

2 Top crust with chicken and olives; sprinkle with feta and mozzarella cheeses.

3 Bake about 10 minutes longer or until cheese is melted. Sprinkle with tomato and cucumber.

1 Serving: Calories 300 (Calories from Fat 125); Total Fat 14g (Saturated Fat 6g); Cholesterol 30mg; Sodium 1140mg; Total Carbohydrate 28g (Dietary Fiber 1g); Protein 15g

fajita pizza

Prep Time: 20 min ▪ **Start to Finish:** 30 min ▪ 6 Servings

2 tablespoons vegetable oil

$^1/_2$ lb boneless skinless chicken breasts, cut into $^1/_8$- to $^1/_2$-inch strips

$^1/_2$ medium bell pepper, cut into thin strips

1 small onion, sliced

$^1/_2$ cup chunky-style salsa or picante sauce

$1^1/_2$ cups Original Bisquick mix

$^1/_3$ cup very hot water

$1^1/_2$ cups shredded mozzarella cheese (6 oz)

1 Move oven rack to lowest position. Heat oven to 450°F. Grease 12-inch pizza pan with shortening or butter. Heat 10-inch skillet over medium-high heat. Add oil; rotate skillet to coat bottom and side. Cook chicken in oil 3 minutes, stirring frequently. Stir in bell pepper and onion. Cook 3 to 4 minutes, stirring frequently, until vegetables are crisp and chicken is no longer pink in center; remove from heat. Stir in salsa; set aside.

2 In medium bowl stir together Bisquick and very hot water until soft dough forms; beat vigorously with spoon 20 strokes. Press dough in pizza pan, using fingers dipped in Bisquick mix; pinch edge to form $^1/_2$-inch rim. Sprinkle $^3/_4$ cup of the cheese over crust. Top with chicken mixture. Sprinkle with remaining $^3/_4$ cup cheese.

3 Bake about 12 minutes or until crust is brown and cheese is melted and bubbly.

1 Serving: Calories 295 (Calories from Fat 135); Total Fat 15g (Saturated Fat 5g); Cholesterol 40mg; Sodium 690mg; Total Carbohydrate 22g (Dietary Fiber 1g); Protein 19g

4
hearty soups

asian beef and noodle soup

Prep Time: 1 hr 10 min ▪ **Start to Finish:** 1 hr 10 min ▪ 6 Servings

3 oz uncooked cellophane noodles (bean threads)

1 tablespoon dark sesame oil

1 1/2 lb boneless beef top sirloin steak, cut into bite-size strips

2 teaspoons finely chopped garlic

2 packages (3.5 oz each) fresh shiitake or button mushrooms, sliced

6 cups beef broth

2 cups finely sliced bok choy

1 cup julienne (matchstick-cut) carrots

1/2 teaspoon salt

1/2 teaspoon ground ginger

1/8 teaspoon pepper

2 medium green onions, sliced (2 tablespoons)

1 In medium bowl, soak bundle of cellophane noodles in warm water 10 to 15 minutes or until softened; drain. Cut noodle bundle into thirds. Cover and set aside.

2 In 5- to 6-quart Dutch oven, heat oil over medium-high heat. Cook beef, garlic and mushrooms in oil 5 to 6 minutes, stirring occasionally, just until beef is no longer pink.

3 Stir in remaining ingredients except noodles and onions. Heat to boiling; reduce heat to medium-low. Cover and cook 14 to 15 minutes, stirring occasionally, until beef is tender.

4 Stir in noodles. Cover and cook 2 to 3 minutes or until noodles are hot. Sprinkle with onions.

1 Serving: Calories 235 (Calories from Fat 65); Total Fat 7g (Saturated Fat 2g); Cholesterol 60mg; Sodium 1300mg; Total Carbohydrate 14g (Dietary Fiber 2g); Protein 28g

A salad of pink grapefruit sections, sliced seeded cucumbers and sliced celery tossed with your favorite Asian dressing goes great with this noodle soup dinner. Try topping the salad with rice crackers for extra crunch.

italian chicken noodle soup

Prep Time: 35 min ▪ **Start to Finish:** 35 min ▪ 6 Servings

1 tablespoon olive or vegetable oil

2 boneless skinless chicken breasts (about ¹/₂ lb), cut into ¹/₂-inch pieces

1 medium onion, chopped (¹/₂ cup)

2 cans (14 oz each) chicken broth

2 cups water

3 medium carrots, sliced (1¹/₂ cups)

2 cups broccoli florets

1¹/₂ cups uncooked medium egg noodles

1 teaspoon dried basil leaves

¹/₂ teaspoon garlic-pepper blend

¹/₄ cup shredded Parmesan cheese

1 In 4-quart saucepan, heat oil over medium heat. Add chicken. Cook 4 to 6 minutes, stirring occasionally, until no longer pink in center. Stir in onion. Cook 2 to 3 minutes, stirring occasionally, until onion is tender.

2 Stir in broth, water and carrots. Heat to boiling. Cook 5 minutes over medium heat. Stir in broccoli, noodles, basil and garlic-pepper blend. Heat to boiling; reduce heat. Simmer uncovered 8 to 10 minutes, stirring occasionally, until vegetables and noodles are tender.

3 Top each serving with cheese.

1 Serving (1¹/₂ cups): Calories 170 (Calories from Fat 50); Total Fat 6g (Saturated Fat 2g); Cholesterol 35mg; Sodium 710mg; Total Carbohydrate 13g (Dietary Fiber 2g); Protein 15g

Sweet, earthy parsnips are cousins to carrots, celery and parsley and they look like large white carrots. Give them a try!

tortellini soup

Prep Time: 40 min ▪ **Start to Finish:** 40 min ▪ 5 Servings

2 tablespoons butter or margarine
1 medium stalk celery, chopped (¹/₂ cup)
1 medium carrot, chopped (¹/₂ cup)
1 small onion, chopped (¹/₄ cup)
1 clove garlic, finely chopped
6 cups water
2 extra-large vegetarian vegetable bouillon cubes
2¹/₂ cups dried cheese-filled tortellini (10 oz)
1 tablespoon chopped fresh parsley
¹/₂ teaspoon ground nutmeg
¹/₄ teaspoon pepper
Freshly grated Parmesan cheese, if desired

1 In 4-quart Dutch oven, melt butter over medium heat. Add celery, carrot, onion and garlic; cook, stirring frequently, until crisp-tender.

2 Stir in water and bouillon cubes. Heat to boiling. Reduce heat to low; stir in tortellini. Cover; simmer about 20 minutes, stirring occasionally, until tortellini are tender.

3 Stir in parsley, nutmeg and pepper. Sprinkle individual servings with cheese.

1 Serving: Calories 280 (Calories from Fat 90); Total Fat 10g (Saturated Fat 5g); Cholesterol 55mg; Sodium 1420mg; Total Carbohydrate 38g (Dietary Fiber 2g); Protein 11g

chicken tortilla soup

Prep Time: 35 min ▪ **Start to Finish:** 35 min ▪ 6 Servings

1 carton (32 oz) chicken broth
1 cup chunky-style salsa (from 16-oz jar)
2 cups shredded deli rotisserie chicken (from 2- to 2¹/₂-lb chicken)
³/₄ cup crushed tortilla chips
1 medium avocado, pitted, peeled and chopped
1¹/₂ cups shredded Monterey Jack cheese (6 oz)
2 tablespoons chopped fresh cilantro
Lime wedges, if desired

1 In 3-quart saucepan, heat broth, salsa and chicken to boiling over medium-high heat, stirring occasionally.

2 Meanwhile, divide crushed chips among 6 serving bowls. Spoon hot soup over chips, then top with avocado, cheese and cilantro. Serve with lime wedges.

1 Serving: Calories 330 (Calories from Fat 180); Total Fat 20g (Saturated Fat 8g); Cholesterol 65mg; Sodium 1390mg; Total Carbohydrate 13g (Dietary Fiber 2g); Protein 24g

Adjust the heat level to individual tastes by choosing mild or medium salsa.

noodle and chicken bowls

Prep Time: 15 min ∎ **Start to Finish:** 15 min ∎ 4 Servings

4 cups water

2 packages (3 oz each) Oriental-flavor ramen noodle soup mix

1 cup fresh spinach leaves, torn into bite-size pieces

2 oz fresh snow pea pods, strings removed, cut in half crosswise ($^1/_2$ cup)

$^1/_2$ cup shredded or julienne (matchstick-cut) carrots

1 can (8 oz) sliced water chestnuts, drained

1 teaspoon sesame oil

$1^1/_2$ cups chopped deli rotisserie chicken (from 2- to $2^1/_2$-lb chicken)

2 medium green onions, chopped (2 tablespoons)

1 In 3-quart saucepan, heat water to boiling over medium-high heat. Add noodles (breaking apart if desired), spinach, pea pods, carrots and water chestnuts. Cook 3 minutes, stirring occasionally.

2 Stir in seasoning packets from soup mixes, sesame oil, chicken and onions. Cook 1 to 2 minutes or until chicken is hot.

1 Serving: Calories 330 (Calories from Fat 120); Total Fat 13g (Saturated Fat 4g); Cholesterol 45mg; Sodium 940mg; Total Carbohydrate 34g (Dietary Fiber 4g); Protein 20g

Scatter chopped fresh basil, mint and/or cilantro over the soup just before serving for a fresh taste similar to traditional Vietnamese pho noodle bowls.

chicken-vegetable pot pie soup

Prep Time: 1 hr ▪ **Start to Finish:** 1 hr ▪ 6 Servings

1 sheet frozen puff pastry (from 17.3-oz package), thawed

2 tablespoons butter or margarine

6 small red potatoes, cut into eighths

1 medium stalk celery, coarsely chopped ($^1/_2$ cup)

1 medium carrot, coarsely chopped ($^1/_2$ cup)

1 small onion, coarsely chopped ($^1/_4$ cup)

5 cups chicken broth

$^1/_4$ cup quick-mixing flour

1 teaspoon poultry seasoning

$^1/_4$ teaspoon salt

$^1/_8$ teaspoon pepper

2$^1/_2$ cups 1-inch pieces deli rotisserie chicken (from 2- to 2$^1/_2$-lb chicken)

1 cup frozen sweet peas (from 1-lb bag)

$^1/_4$ cup whipping cream

1 Heat oven to 400°F. Cut 6 rounds from puff pastry with 3-inch round cutter. Place on ungreased cookie sheet. Bake 12 to 15 minutes or until puffed and golden brown. Keep warm.

2 Meanwhile, in 4 ½- to 5-quart Dutch oven, melt butter over medium-high heat. Cook potatoes, celery, carrot and onion in butter 5 to 6 minutes, stirring frequently, until onion is softened.

3 Beat broth, flour, poultry seasoning, salt and pepper into potato mixture with whisk. Heat to boiling; reduce heat to medium-low. Cover; cook 15 to 20 minutes, stirring occasionally, until potatoes are tender and soup is slightly thickened.

4 Stir in remaining ingredients. Cover; cook 5 to 6 minutes, stirring occasionally, until chicken and peas are hot. Ladle soup into bowls; top each serving with pastry.

1 Serving: Calories 340 (Calories from Fat 120); Total Fat 13g (Saturated Fat 6g); Cholesterol 75mg; Sodium 1310mg; Total Carbohydrate 32g (Dietary Fiber 4g); Protein 25g

Save time! Pick up the small amounts of carrot and celery at the salad bar in your grocery store.

italian tomato soup with pesto-cheese toasts

Prep Time: 15 min ∎ **Start to Finish:** 15 min ∎ 4 Servings

1 cup water
2 cans (14 oz each) diced tomatoes with Italian herbs, undrained
1 can (11.5 oz) tomato juice
4 slices rosemary, Italian or French bread, 1/2 inch thick
2 tablespoons basil pesto
2 tablespoons shredded Parmesan cheese

1 In 3-quart saucepan, heat water, tomatoes and tomato juice to boiling.

2 Set oven control to broil. Place bread on ungreased cookie sheet. Spread with pesto; sprinkle with cheese. With tops 4 to 6 inches from heat, broil 1 to 2 minutes or until edges of bread are golden brown.

3 Into 4 soup bowls, ladle soup. Top each serving with bread slice.

1 Serving: Calories 260 (Calories from Fat 60); Total Fat 7g (Saturated Fat 2g); Cholesterol 0mg; Sodium 910mg; Total Carbohydrate 39g (Dietary Fiber 4g); Protein 9g

Take creative license! Turn this into a pizza soup by stirring in 1 lb browned (drained) Italian sausage and a 2 1/2-oz can of sliced mushrooms (drained) in step 1. Add a simple tossed salad with dressing, and you're good to go.

chunky tomato soup

Prep Time: 1 hr 35 min ▪ **Start to Finish:** 1 hr 35 min ▪ 8 Servings

2 tablespoons olive or vegetable oil

2 cloves garlic, finely chopped

2 medium stalks celery, coarsely chopped (1 cup)

2 medium carrots, coarsely chopped (1 cup)

2 cans (28 oz each) plum (Roma) tomatoes, undrained

2 cups water

1 teaspoon dried basil leaves

$^1/_2$ teaspoon pepper

2 cans (14 oz each) chicken broth

1 In 5- to 6-quart Dutch oven, heat oil over medium-high heat. Cook garlic, celery and carrots in oil 5 to 7 minutes, stirring frequently, until carrots are crisp-tender.

2 Stir in tomatoes, breaking up tomatoes coarsely. Stir in water, basil, pepper and broth. Heat to boiling; reduce heat to low.

3 Cover and simmer 1 hour, stirring occasionally.

1 Serving: Calories 95 (Calories from Fat 35); Total Fat 4g (Saturated Fat 1g); Cholesterol 0mg; Sodium 760mg; Total Carbohydrate 11g (Dietary Fiber 3g); Protein 4g

Hot grilled Cheddar cheese sandwiches make a great partner for this veggie soup. Tall glasses of ice-cold milk and a couple of chocolate chip cookies are all you need to serve up lunch!

minestrone with garlic croutons

Prep Time: 45 min ▪ **Start to Finish:** 45 min ▪ 6 Servings

Croutons

2 cups cubed ($^1/_2$ to $^3/_4$ inch) French bread

$^1/_4$ cup butter or margarine, melted

$^1/_2$ teaspoon garlic powder

$^1/_4$ teaspoon seasoned salt

Soup

1 tablespoon olive or vegetable oil

1$^1/_2$ cups frozen bell pepper and onion stir-fry (from 1-lb bag)

2 cups frozen mixed vegetables (from 1-lb bag)

2 cans (14.5 oz each) Italian-style stewed tomatoes, undrained

2 cans (14 oz each) beef broth

$^1/_2$ cup uncooked small pasta shells (2 oz)

1 can (15 oz) dark red kidney beans, drained, rinsed

1 Heat oven to 350°F. In medium bowl, mix all crouton ingredients until bread is well coated. In ungreased 15×10×1-inch pan, spread croutons. Bake 15 to 20 minutes, stirring and turning occasionally, until golden brown and crispy.

2 Meanwhile, in 4-quart saucepan, heat oil over medium-high heat. Add stir-fry vegetables. Cook 3 to 4 minutes, stirring frequently, until tender. Stir in mixed vegetables, tomatoes and broth. Heat to boiling, breaking up tomatoes with spoon as mixture cooks. Stir in pasta. Cook uncovered over medium heat 10 to 12 minutes, stirring occasionally, until vegetables and pasta are tender.

3 Stir in beans. Cook 4 to 5 minutes, stirring occasionally, until thoroughly heated. Top each serving with warm croutons.

1 Serving: Calories 350 (Calories from Fat 100); Total Fat 11g (Saturated Fat 5g); Cholesterol 20mg; Sodium 1330mg; Total Carbohydrate 50g (Dietary Fiber 8g); Protein 13g

Fresh croutons are wonderful, but if you don't feel like making them, use purchased garlic or Parmesan croutons instead. For a heartier soup, you can add cooked Italian sausage or diced cooked beef with the beans.

minestrone with italian sausage

Prep Time: 45 min ∎ **Start to Finish:** 45 min ∎ 7 Servings

1 tablespoon olive or vegetable oil

1 lb bulk sweet Italian sausage

1 medium onion, chopped ($^1/_2$ cup)

2 medium carrots, coarsely chopped (1 cup)

2 teaspoons dried basil leaves

2 teaspoons finely chopped garlic

3 cans (14 oz each) beef broth

1 can (14.5 oz) diced tomatoes, undrained

1 can (15.5 oz) great northern beans, rinsed and drained

1 cup uncooked small elbow macaroni (3.5 oz)

1 medium zucchini, cut lengthwise in half, then cut into $^1/_4$-inch slices (1 cup)

1 cup frozen cut green beans (from 1-lb bag)

1 In 5-quart Dutch oven, heat oil over medium-high heat. Cook sausage, onion, carrots, basil and garlic in oil 5 to 7 minutes, stirring frequently, until sausage is no longer pink; drain.

2 Stir broth, tomatoes and great northern beans into sausage mixture. Heat to boiling; reduce heat to medium-low. Cover and cook 7 to 8 minutes, stirring occasionally.

3 Stir in macaroni, zucchini and green beans; heat to boiling. Cook over medium-high heat 5 to 6 minutes, stirring occasionally, until vegetables are hot and macaroni is tender.

1 Serving: Calories 345 (Calories from Fat 135); Total Fat 15g (Saturated Fat 5g); Cholesterol 35mg; Sodium 1060mg; Total Carbohydrate 37g (Dietary Fiber 6g); Protein 21g

Make it meatless! Simply substitute an additional can of great northern beans or your favorite canned beans for the sausage, and use vegetable broth instead of beef broth.

southwest black bean soup

Prep Time: 30 min ∎ **Start to Finish:** 30 min ∎ 6 Servings

1 tablespoon olive or canola oil

1 medium onion, chopped

2 cloves garlic, finely chopped

1 to 2 jalapeño chiles, seeded, finely chopped

2 cans (15 oz each) black beans, rinsed, drained

1 can (14.5 oz) organic diced or fire-roasted diced tomatoes, undrained

1 can (14 oz) reduced-sodium chicken broth or vegetable broth

2 teaspoons ground cumin

2 tablespoons chopped fresh cilantro

Plain yogurt or reduced-fat sour cream, if desired

Lime wedges, if desired

1 In 4-quart saucepan, heat oil over medium heat. Add onion, garlic and chiles; cook 3 to 4 minutes, stirring occasionally, until tender.

2 Stir in beans, tomatoes, broth and cumin. Heat to boiling over high heat. Reduce heat to medium-low; cover and simmer 15 minutes. Remove from heat. Using a potato masher, mash beans until soup reaches desired consistency. Stir in cilantro. Top individual servings with yogurt and serve with lime wedges, if desired.

1 Serving: Calories 240 (Calories from Fat 30); Total Fat 3g (Saturated Fat 0g); Cholesterol 0mg; Sodium 470mg; Total Carbohydrate 41g (Dietary Fiber 14g); Protein 12g

Black beans are loaded with fiber—the soluble kind that helps to lower blood cholesterol.

cheesy chicken and ham chowder

Prep Time: 20 min ▪ **Start to Finish:** 20 min ▪ 4 Servings

2 cans (18.5 oz each) ready-to-serve russet potatoes and broccoli chowder
1 cup cubed cooked chicken breast
1 cup diced cooked ham
1 cup shredded Cheddar cheese (4 oz)

1 In 3-quart saucepan, heat chowder, chicken and ham over medium-high heat 5 minutes, stirring occasionally.

2 Slowly stir in cheese. Cook about 2 minutes, stirring frequently, until cheese is melted.

1 Serving: Calories 410 (Calories from Fat 220); Total Fat 24g (Saturated Fat 10g); Cholesterol 90mg; Sodium 1620mg; Total Carbohydrate 18g (Dietary Fiber 2g); Protein 30g

Leftover chopped rotisserie chicken works well for the cubed chicken breast. Try pairing different meats and cheeses to come up with a delicious new creation every time.

seafood chowder

Prep Time: 25 min ▪ **Start to Finish:** 25 min ▪ 8 Servings

$1/3$ **cup butter or margarine**

$1/3$ **cup all-purpose flour**

2 cans (14 oz each) chicken broth

4 cups (1 quart) half-and-half

$1/2$ **cup dry white wine or water**

$1/2$ **cup chopped drained roasted red bell peppers (from 7-oz jar)**

12 oz cod fillet, cut into 1-inch pieces

12 oz uncooked deveined peeled medium shrimp, thawed if frozen

$1/2$ **cup basil pesto**

$1/4$ **teaspoon salt**

$1/8$ **teaspoon freshly ground pepper**

1 In 4-quart Dutch oven, melt butter over medium-high heat. Stir in flour. Gradually stir in broth, half-and-half and wine. Stir in bell peppers and cod. Heat to boiling, stirring occasionally.

2 Stir in shrimp. Simmer uncovered 2 to 3 minutes or until shrimp are pink. Stir in pesto, salt and pepper.

1 Serving: Calories 420 (Calories from Fat 280); Total Fat 31g (Saturated Fat 15g); Cholesterol 150mg; Sodium 860mg; Total Carbohydrate 11g (Dietary Fiber 0g); Protein 22g

Cooked shrimp works great in this recipe, too. Just add the shrimp to the chowder and simmer until heated through. As you dish up the soup, sprinkle chopped fresh basil leaves and a little freshly shredded Parmesan cheese on each serving. Or for a simple yet "showy" garnish for each serving, tie a chive around an additional cooked shrimp.

creamy corn and broccoli chowder

Prep Time: 30 min ▪ **Start to Finish:** 30 min ▪ 6 Servings

2 tablespoons butter or margarine
1 medium onion, chopped ($^1/_2$ cup)
1 clove garlic, finely chopped
3 tablespoons all-purpose flour
$^1/_2$ teaspoon coarse salt (kosher or sea salt)
$^1/_8$ teaspoon pepper
3 cups reduced-sodium chicken broth or vegetable broth
1 bag (1 lb) frozen broccoli cuts
2 cups frozen sweet corn (from 1-lb bag)
1 cup half-and-half

1 In 4-quart saucepan, melt butter over medium heat. Cook onion and garlic in butter 2 to 3 minutes, stirring frequently, until tender. Stir in flour, salt and pepper. Cook, stirring constantly, 1 minute.

2 Stir in broth, broccoli and corn. Heat to boiling over high heat. Reduce heat; simmer 5 to 7 minutes, stirring occasionally, until vegetables are tender.

3 Stir in half-and-half. Cook 2 to 3 minutes, stirring occasionally, until hot (do not boil).

1 Serving: Calories 190 (Calories from Fat 80); Total Fat 9g (Saturated Fat 5g); Cholesterol 25mg; Sodium 530mg; Total Carbohydrate 21g (Dietary Fiber 4g); Protein 7g

Just add your favorite crusty bread, sliced cheeses and fresh fruit to complete the meal.

vegetarian chili with spicy tortilla strips

Prep Time: 10 min ▪ **Start to Finish:** 6 hr 20 min ▪ 6 Servings

Spicy Tortilla Strips
3 corn tortillas (6 inch)

1 tablespoon vegetable oil

Dash of ground red pepper (cayenne)

Chili
1 can (15 to 16 oz) dark red kidney beans, drained

1 can (15 to 16 oz) spicy chili beans, undrained

1 can (15 oz) pinquito beans, undrained

1 can (14.5 oz) chili-style chunky tomatoes, undrained

1 large onion, chopped (1 cup)

2 to 3 teaspoons chili powder

¹/₈ teaspoon ground red pepper (cayenne)

1 Heat oven to 375°F. Brush both sides of tortillas with oil. Lightly sprinkle red pepper on one side of tortillas. Cut into ¹/₂-inch strips. Place in single layer on ungreased cookie sheet. Bake 10 to 12 minutes or until strips are crisp and edges are light brown.

2 Meanwhile, in 3¹/₂- to 4-quart slow cooker, mix chili ingredients.

3 Cover and cook on low heat setting 5 to 6 hours or until flavors have blended. Stir well before serving. Top each serving with tortilla strips.

1 Serving: Calories 255 (Calories from Fat 10); Total Fat 1g (Saturated Fat 0g); Cholesterol 0mg; Sodium 1010mg; Total Carbohydrate 59g (Dietary Fiber 15g); Protein 17g

Pinquitos are small, tender pink beans. If your supermarket doesn't carry them, just substitute pinto beans.

chicken enchilada chili

Prep Time: 10 min ▪ **Start to Finish:** 7 hr 10 min ▪ 6 Servings

1¼ lb boneless skinless chicken thighs

1 medium onion, chopped (½ cup)

1 medium yellow or green bell pepper, chopped (1 cup)

2 cans (14.5 oz each) stewed tomatoes with garlic and onion, undrained

2 cans (15 to 16 oz each) chili beans in sauce, undrained

1 can (10 oz) enchilada sauce

⅓ cup sour cream

2 tablespoons chopped fresh cilantro

1 Spray 4- to 5-quart slow cooker with cooking spray. In cooker, mix all ingredients except sour cream and cilantro.

2 Cover and cook on Low heat setting 7 to 8 hours.

3 Stir mixture to break up chicken. Top each serving with cilantro and sour cream.

1 Serving: Calories 340 (Calories from Fat 100); Total Fat 11g (Saturated Fat 4g); Cholesterol 65mg; Sodium 1700mg; Total Carbohydrate 38g (Dietary Fiber 8g); Protein 30g

For super-quick dinners and totable lunches, freeze the chili in single-serving freezer containers. Thaw, then heat in the microwave on High for 4 to 5 minutes, stirring once or twice, until hot.

white bean–chicken chili

Prep Time: 20 min ▪ **Start to Finish:** 20 min ▪ 6 Servings

2 tablespoons butter or margarine

1 large onion, coarsely chopped (1 cup)

2 cloves garlic, finely chopped

3 cups cubed deli rotisserie chicken (from 2- to 2½-lb chicken)

½ teaspoon ground cumin

2 cans (10 oz each) diced tomatoes with green chiles, undrained

1 can (15.5 oz) great northern beans, drained, rinsed

Sour cream, if desired

Chopped fresh cilantro, if desired

1 In 4½- to 5-quart Dutch oven, melt butter over medium-high heat. Cook onion and garlic in butter, stirring occasionally, until onion is tender.

2 Stir in remaining ingredients except sour cream and cilantro. Heat to boiling; reduce heat to low. Simmer uncovered 2 to 3 minutes, stirring occasionally, until hot.

3 Top each serving with sour cream; sprinkle with cilantro.

1 Serving: Calories 280 (Calories from Fat 80); Total Fat 9g (Saturated Fat 4g); Cholesterol 70mg; Sodium 650mg; Total Carbohydrate 23g (Dietary Fiber 6g); Protein 27g

Instead of crackers, serve this chili with tortilla chips for a little crunch.

5
new twists on chicken

southwestern chicken scaloppine

Prep Time: 30 min ▪ **Start to Finish:** 30 min ▪ 4 Servings

4 boneless skinless chicken breasts (about 1¼ lb)
¼ cup all-purpose flour
1 teaspoon ground cumin
¼ teaspoon salt
2 tablespoons vegetable oil
¼ cup chicken broth
¼ teaspoon red pepper sauce, if desired
2 tablespoons lime juice
2 tablespoons chopped fresh cilantro

1 Between pieces of plastic wrap or waxed paper, place chicken breast with smooth side down; gently pound with flat side of meat mallet or rolling pin until about ¼ inch thick. Repeat with remaining chicken. Cut chicken into smaller pieces if desired.

2 In shallow dish, mix flour, cumin and salt. Coat chicken with flour mixture. Reserve 1 teaspoon flour mixture.

3 In 12-inch nonstick skillet, heat oil over medium heat. Add chicken; cook 3 to 5 minutes on each side or until golden brown and no longer pink in center. Remove chicken from skillet; cover to keep warm.

4 In small bowl, stir reserved 1 teaspoon flour mixture into broth. Gradually stir broth mixture and red pepper sauce into skillet. Heat to boiling; stir in lime juice and cilantro. Serve sauce over chicken.

1 Serving: Calories 260 (Calories from Fat 110); Total Fat 12g (Saturated Fat 2.5g); Cholesterol 85mg; Sodium 500mg; Total Carbohydrate 7g (Dietary Fiber 0g); Protein 33g

zesty roasted chicken and potatoes

Prep Time: 10 min ▪ **Start to Finish:** 45 min ▪ 6 Servings

6 boneless skinless chicken breasts (about 1²/₃ lb)

1 lb small red potatoes, cut into fourths

¹/₃ cup mayonnaise or salad dressing

3 tablespoons Dijon mustard

¹/₂ teaspoon pepper

2 cloves garlic, finely chopped

Chopped fresh chives, if desired

1 Heat oven to 350°F. Spray 15×10×1-inch pan with cooking spray.

2 Place chicken and potatoes in pan. In small bowl, mix remaining ingredients except chives; brush over chicken and potatoes.

3 Bake uncovered 30 to 35 minutes or until potatoes are tender and juice of chicken is clear when center of thickest part is cut. Sprinkle with chives.

1 Serving: Calories 380 (Calories from Fat 210); Total Fat 23g (Saturated Fat 5g); Cholesterol 95mg; Sodium 340mg; Total Carbohydrate 14g (Dietary Fiber 2g); Protein 28g

Want to make this lighter? Use low-fat mayonnaise for 9 grams of fat and 270 calories per serving.

chicken marsala

Prep Time: 45 min ▪ **Start to Finish:** 45 min ▪ 4 Servings

¼ **cup all-purpose flour**

¼ **teaspoon salt**

¼ **teaspoon pepper**

4 boneless skinless chicken breasts (about 1¼ lb)

2 tablespoons olive or vegetable oil

2 cloves garlic, finely chopped

1 cup sliced mushrooms (3 lb)

¼ **cup chopped fresh parsley or 1 tablespoon parsley flakes**

½ **cup dry Marsala wine or chicken broth**

1 In shallow bowl, mix flour, salt and pepper. Coat chicken with flour mixture; shake off excess flour.

2 In 10-inch skillet, heat oil over medium-high heat. Cook garlic, mushrooms and parsley in oil 5 minutes, stirring frequently.

3 Add chicken to skillet. Cook uncovered about 8 minutes, turning once, until chicken is brown. Add wine. Cook uncovered 8 to 10 minutes, turning once, until juice of chicken is clear when center of thickest part is cut (170°F).

1 Serving: Calories 290 (Calories from Fat 100); Total Fat 11g (Saturated Fat 2g); Cholesterol 85mg; Sodium 230mg; Total Carbohydrate 11g (Dietary Fiber 1g); Protein 33g

You can substitute dry sherry for the Marsala, if you like. Amber-hued Marsala wine comes from Sicily and tastes similar to sherry. Marsala can be either dry or sweet, the dry used for savory dishes and the sweet usually for desserts.

dijon chicken smothered in mushrooms

Prep Time: 22 min ▪ **Start to Finish:** 22 min ▪ 4 Servings

4 boneless skinless chicken breasts (about 1¼ lb)

¼ cup all-purpose flour

½ teaspoon salt

¼ teaspoon pepper

2 tablespoons olive or canola oil

½ cup roasted garlic–seasoned chicken broth (from 14-oz can)

1½ tablespoons Dijon mustard

1 jar (4.5 oz) sliced mushrooms, drained

Chopped fresh thyme, if desired

1 Place chicken between 2 sheets of plastic wrap or waxed paper. Flatten chicken to ¼-inch thickness with meat mallet or rolling pin. In shallow dish, mix flour, salt and pepper.

2 In 12-inch nonstick skillet, heat oil over medium-high heat. Coat both sides of chicken with flour mixture. Cook chicken in oil 6 to 8 minutes, turning once, until chicken is no longer pink in center. Remove chicken to serving plate; cover to keep warm.

3 Stir broth into skillet. Heat to boiling over medium-high heat. Stir in mustard and mushrooms. Cook 2 to 3 minutes, stirring frequently, until slightly thickened. Spoon sauce over chicken. Sprinkle with thyme.

1 Serving: Calories 210 (Calories from Fat 60); Total Fat 7g (Saturated Fat 1.5g); Cholesterol 70mg; Sodium 630mg; Total Carbohydrate 9g (Dietary Fiber 0g); Protein 28g

chicken in fresh herbs

Prep Time: 30 min ■ **Start to Finish:** 30 min ■ 4 Servings

4 boneless skinless chicken breasts (about 1¹/₄ lb)
1 medium shallot, chopped
¹/₄ cup chopped fresh chervil leaves
¹/₄ cup chopped fresh tarragon leaves
¹/₂ cup dry white wine or chicken broth
1 tablespoon lemon juice
¹/₂ teaspoon salt
Cracked pepper, if desired

1 Heat 10-inch skillet over medium-high heat until hot.

2 Cook all ingredients except pepper in skillet 15 to 20 minutes, turning chicken once, until juice of chicken is clear when center of thickest part is cut (170°F). Sprinkle with pepper.

1 Serving: Calories 170 (Calories from Fat 40); Total Fat 4.5g (Saturated Fat 1.5g); Cholesterol 85mg; Sodium 380mg; Total Carbohydrate 0g (Dietary Fiber 0g); Protein 31g

cornmeal chicken with fresh peach salsa

Prep Time: 30 min ▮ **Start to Finish:** 30 min ▮ 4 Servings

Salsa
3 cups chopped peeled peaches

1 large tomato, chopped (1 cup)

$^1/_4$ cup chopped fresh cilantro

3 tablespoons vegetable oil

2 tablespoons white vinegar

$^1/_4$ teaspoon salt

Chicken
$^1/_2$ cup yellow cornmeal

$^1/_2$ teaspoon salt

$^1/_2$ teaspoon pepper

4 boneless skinless chicken breasts (about $1^1/_4$ lb)

2 tablespoons vegetable oil

1 In large bowl, mix salsa ingredients.

2 In shallow bowl, mix cornmeal, salt and pepper. Coat chicken with cornmeal mixture.

3 In 10-inch skillet, heat oil over medium-high heat. Cook chicken in oil 15 to 20 minutes, turning once, until juice is no longer pink when center of thickest part is cut (170°F). Top with salsa.

1 Serving: Calories 400 (Calories from Fat 180); Total Fat 20g (Saturated Fat 3g); Cholesterol 75mg; Sodium 510mg; Total Carbohydrate 31g (Dietary Fiber 5g); Protein 29g

moroccan spiced chicken

Prep Time: 30 min ▪ **Start to Finish:** 30 min ▪ 4 Servings

1 tablespoon paprika
$^1/_2$ teaspoon salt
$^1/_2$ teaspoon ground cumin
$^1/_4$ teaspoon ground allspice
$^1/_4$ teaspoon ground cinnamon
4 boneless skinless chicken breasts (about $1^1/_4$ lb)
1 tablespoon vegetable oil
2 cups water
1 teaspoon vegetable oil
$1^1/_2$ cups uncooked couscous
$^1/_4$ cup raisins, if desired
1 small papaya, peeled, seeded and sliced

1 In small bowl, mix paprika, salt, cumin, allspice and cinnamon. Coat both sides of chicken with spice mixture.

2 In 10-inch skillet, heat 1 tablespoon oil over medium heat. Cook chicken in oil 15 to 20 minutes, turning once, until juice of chicken is clear when center of thickest part is cut (170°F).

3 Meanwhile, in 2-quart saucepan, heat water and 1 teaspoon oil just to boiling. Stir in couscous; remove from heat. Cover; let stand 5 minutes. Fluff couscous before serving; stir in raisins. Serve chicken with couscous and papaya.

1 Serving: Calories 470 (Calories from Fat 90); Total Fat 10g (Saturated Fat 2g,); Cholesterol 85mg; Sodium 380mg; Total Carbohydrate 55g (Dietary Fiber 5g); Protein 40g

Round out the meal with warmed pita folds drizzled with olive oil or melted butter or with Middle Eastern flatbread.

indonesian chicken breasts

Prep Time: 35 min ▪ **Start to Finish:** 1 hr 35 min ▪ 4 Servings

$^1/_2$ **cup orange juice**
$^1/_4$ **cup peanut butter**
2 teaspoons curry powder
4 boneless skinless chicken breasts (about 1$^1/_4$ lb)
1 medium red bell pepper, cut in half
$^1/_4$ **cup shredded coconut**
$^1/_4$ **cup currants**
Hot cooked rice, if desired

1 In medium nonmetal bowl, beat orange juice, peanut butter and curry powder, using whisk. Add chicken, turning to coat with marinade. Cover and refrigerate, turning once, at least 1 hour but no longer than 24 hours.

2 Heat gas or charcoal grill. Remove chicken from marinade; discard marinade. Cover and grill chicken and bell pepper 4 to 6 inches from medium heat 15 to 20 minutes, turning once, until juice of chicken is clear when center of thickest part is cut (170°F). To serve, cut chicken breasts diagonally into $^1/_2$-inch slices and bell pepper into $^1/_2$-inch strips. Top chicken and bell pepper with coconut and currants. Serve with rice.

1 Serving: Calories 315 (Calories from Fat 125); Total Fat 14g (Saturated Fat 5g); Cholesterol 70mg; Sodium 160mg; Total Carbohydrate 19g (Dietary Fiber 2g); Protein 30g

provolone-smothered chicken

Prep Time: 25 min ▪ **Start to Finish:** 55 min ▪ 4 Servings

4 boneless skinless chicken breasts (about 1¹/₄ lb)
¹/₂ cup zesty Italian dressing
¹/₂ teaspoon garlic pepper blend
2 tablespoons chopped fresh basil leaves
4 thin slices tomato
4 slices (¹/₂ to ²/₃ oz each) provolone cheese

1 Place chicken in shallow dish. Pour dressing over chicken. Cover and refrigerate about 30 minutes.

2 Heat closed medium-size contact grill for 5 minutes. Remove chicken from marinade; reserve marinade. Sprinkle chicken with garlic pepper blend. Place chicken on grill. Close grill. Grill 4 to 6 minutes, brushing with marinade once, until juice of chicken is no longer pink when center of thickest part is cut (170°F). Discard remaining marinade.

3 Sprinkle each chicken breast with basil; top with tomato and cheese. Let stand on grill 3 to 5 minutes or until cheese is melted.

1 Serving: Calories 250 (Calories from Fat 100); Total Fat 11g (Saturated Fat 4g); Cholesterol 95mg; Sodium 270mg; Total Carbohydrate 2g (Dietary Fiber 0g); Protein 35g

Serve the cheese-topped chicken on toasted French bread slices with lettuce and sliced red onion.

grilled cheddar-stuffed chicken breasts

Prep Time: 30 min ▪ **Start to Finish:** 30 min ▪ 4 Servings

4 boneless skinless chicken breasts (about 1¼ lb)
¼ teaspoon salt
¼ teaspoon pepper
1 piece (3 oz) Cheddar cheese
1 tablespoon butter or margarine, melted
¼ cup chunky-style salsa

1 Heat gas or charcoal grill. Between pieces of plastic wrap or waxed paper, place each chicken breast smooth side down; gently pound with flat side of meat mallet or rolling pin until about ¼ inch thick. Sprinkle with salt and pepper.

2 Cut cheese into 4 slices, about 3×1×¼ inch. Place 1 slice cheese on center of each chicken piece. Roll chicken around cheese, folding in sides. Brush rolls with butter.

3 Place chicken rolls, seam sides down, on grill. Cover grill; cook over medium heat about 15 minutes, turning after 10 minutes, until chicken is no longer pink in center. Serve with salsa.

1 Serving: Calories 280 (Calories from Fat 130); Total Fat 15g (Saturated Fat 8g); Cholesterol 115mg; Sodium 450mg; Total Carbohydrate 1g (Dietary Fiber 0g); Protein 37g

Add a peppery punch to this easy chicken dish by using Monterey Jack cheese with jalapeño chiles instead of the Cheddar cheese.

french peasant chicken stew

Prep Time: 30 min ■ **Start to Finish:** 30 min ■ 6 Servings

2 cups ready-to-eat baby-cut carrots
1 cup sliced fresh mushrooms (about 3 oz)
4 small red potatoes, cut into quarters
1 jar (12 oz) chicken gravy
1 can (14 oz) reduced-sodium chicken broth
1 teaspoon dried thyme leaves
1/2 cup frozen baby sweet peas
1 deli rotisserie chicken (2 to 2 1/2 lb), cut into serving pieces

1 In 4-quart saucepan, mix all ingredients except peas and chicken.

2 Heat to boiling over medium-high heat. Reduce heat to medium-low. Cover; simmer about 20 minutes or until vegetables are tender.

3 Stir in peas and chicken. Cover; simmer about 5 minutes or until peas are tender.

1 Serving: Calories 290 (Calories from Fat 90); Total Fat 10g (Saturated Fat 3g); Cholesterol 75mg; Sodium 920mg; Total Carbohydrate 22g (Dietary Fiber 4g); Protein 28g

For a quick Coq au Vin, add 2 tablespoons of white wine.

lemon-basil chicken and vegetables

Prep Time: 30 min ▌ **Start to Finish:** 30 min ▌ 4 Servings

1 cup uncooked brown or white rice

1 lb boneless skinless chicken breasts

¹⁄₄ teaspoon coarsely ground pepper

¹⁄₄ teaspoon garlic powder

1 medium onion, cut into thin wedges

1 bag (1 lb) frozen baby bean and carrot blend (or other combination)

³⁄₄ cup water

¹⁄₂ cup lemon-basil stir-fry sauce

1 teaspoon cornstarch

1 Cook rice as directed on package. While rice is cooking, cut chicken into 2×¹⁄₄-inch strips. Spray 12-inch nonstick skillet with cooking spray; heat over medium-high heat. Add chicken to skillet; sprinkle with pepper and garlic powder. Stir-fry 4 to 6 minutes or until brown. Add onion; stir-fry 2 minutes.

2 Stir in frozen vegetables and water. Heat to boiling; reduce heat to medium. Cover and cook 5 to 6 minutes, stirring occasionally, until vegetables are tender.

3 In small bowl, mix stir-fry sauce and cornstarch until smooth; stir into mixture in skillet. Heat to boiling, stirring constantly. Boil and stir 1 minute. Divide rice among 4 bowls. Top with chicken mixture.

1 Serving: Calories 410 (Calories from Fat 65); Total Fat 7g (Saturated Fat 2g); Cholesterol 70mg; Sodium 630mg; Total Carbohydrate 61g (Dietary Fiber 8g); Protein 33g

caesar chicken with orzo

Prep Time: 30 min ∎ **Start to Finish:** 30 min ∎ 4 Servings

1 tablespoon vegetable oil

4 boneless skinless chicken breasts (about 1¼ lb)

1 can (14 oz) chicken broth

1 cup water

1 cup uncooked orzo pasta (6 oz)

1 bag (1 lb) frozen baby whole carrots, green beans and yellow beans (or other combination)

3 tablespoons Caesar dressing

⅛ teaspoon coarsely ground pepper

1 In 10-inch skillet, heat oil over medium-high heat. Cook chicken in oil about 10 minutes, turning once, until brown. Remove chicken from skillet; keep warm.

2 Add broth and water to skillet; heat to boiling. Stir in pasta; heat to boiling. Cook uncovered 8 to 10 minutes, stirring occasionally, until pasta is tender. Stir in frozen vegetables and dressing. Add chicken. Sprinkle with pepper.

3 Heat to boiling; reduce heat. Simmer uncovered about 5 minutes or until vegetables are crisp-tender and juice of chicken is no longer pink when centers of thickest pieces are cut.

1 Serving: Calories 405 (Calories from Fat 115); Total Fat 13g (Saturated Fat 3g); Cholesterol 75mg; Sodium 670mg; Total Carbohydrate 43g (Dietary Fiber 6g); Protein 38g

Use your favorite combo of frozen vegetables here—the prep is so easy!

cheesy chicken and rotini casserole

Prep Time: 15 min ▪ **Start to Finish:** 1 hr ▪ 6 Servings

3 cups uncooked rotini pasta (9 oz)

2 cups cut-up cooked chicken

1 cup frozen onions, celery, bell pepper and parsley (from 16-oz bag)

1 can (10^3/$_4$ oz) condensed cream of chicken soup

1 cup chicken broth

2 plum (Roma) tomatoes, each cut into 6 wedges

3 medium green onions, sliced (3 tablespoons)

^{1}/$_2$ cup shredded Cheddar cheese (2 oz)

1 Heat oven to 350°F. Grease 8-inch square pan. Cook and drain pasta as directed on package.

2 In pan, mix pasta, chicken, frozen vegetables, soup and broth. Bake uncovered 35 to 40 minutes or until bubbly around edges.

3 Top with tomatoes. Sprinkle with onions and cheese. Bake uncovered about 3 minutes or until cheese is melted.

1 Serving: Calories 365 (Calories from Fat 100); Total Fat 11g (Saturated Fat 4g); Cholesterol 50mg; Sodium 760mg; Total Carbohydrate 44g (Dietary Fiber 2g); Protein 25g

Mushroom fans—go ahead and make this casserole with cream of mushroom soup.

mexican chicken–sour cream lasagna

Prep Time: 30 min ▪ **Start to Finish:** 1 hr 45 min ▪ 8 Servings

12 uncooked lasagna noodles
2 cans (10.75 oz each) condensed cream of chicken soup
1 container (8 oz) sour cream
¹/₄ cup milk
1¹/₄ teaspoons ground cumin
¹/₂ teaspoon garlic powder
3 cups cubed cooked chicken (about 1¹/₂ lb)
1 can (4.5 oz) chopped green chiles, undrained
8 to 10 medium green onions, sliced (about ¹/₂ cup)
¹/₂ cup chopped fresh cilantro or parsley
3 cups finely shredded Mexican-style Cheddar–Monterey Jack cheese blend (12 oz)
1 large red bell pepper, chopped (1 cup)
1 can (2.25 oz) sliced ripe olives, drained
1 cup crushed nacho cheese flavor tortilla chips
Additional chopped or whole fresh cilantro leaves, if desired

1 Heat oven to 350°F. Spray bottom and sides of 13×9-inch (3-quart) glass baking dish with cooking spray. Cook and drain noodles as directed on package. Meanwhile, in large bowl, mix soup, sour cream, milk, cumin, garlic powder, chicken and chiles.

2 Spread about 1¹/₄ cups of the chicken mixture in baking dish. Top with 4 noodles. Spread 1¹/₄ cups chicken mixture over noodles; sprinkle with onions and cilantro. Sprinkle with 1 cup of the cheese.

3 Top with 4 noodles. Spread 1¹/₄ cups chicken mixture over noodles; sprinkle with bell pepper and olives. Sprinkle with 1 cup of the cheese. Top with 4 noodles; spread with remaining chicken mixture.

4 Bake uncovered 30 minutes; sprinkle with tortilla chips and remaining 1 cup cheese. Bake 15 to 30 minutes longer or until bubbly and hot in center. Sprinkle with additional cilantro. Let stand 15 minutes before cutting.

1 Serving: Calories 570 (Calories from Fat 280); Total Fat 32g (Saturated Fat 15g); Cholesterol 110mg; Sodium 1150mg; Total Carbohydrate 41g (Dietary Fiber 3g); Protein 33g

Spoon your favorite salsa over the lasagna for a touch of color.

chicken and rice with autumn vegetables

Prep Time: 15 min ▪ **Start to Finish:** 45 min ▪ 4 Servings

1 package (about 6 oz) chicken-flavored rice mix or rice and vermicelli mix
2 cups 1-inch pieces butternut squash
1 medium zucchini, cut lengthwise in half, then crosswise into $2/3$-inch slices
1 medium red bell pepper, cut into 1-inch pieces (1 cup)
4 boneless, skinless chicken breasts (about $1^1/_4$ lb)
2 cups water
$^1/_2$ cup garlic-and-herb spreadable cheese

1 Heat oven to 425°F. In ungreased 13×9-inch pan, mix rice, contents of seasoning packet, squash, zucchini and bell pepper.

2 Spray 10-inch skillet with cooking spray; heat over medium-high heat. Cook chicken in skillet 5 minutes, turning once, until brown. Remove chicken from skillet.

3 Add water to skillet; heat to boiling. Pour boiling water over rice mixture; stir to mix. Stir in cheese. Place chicken on rice mixture.

4 Cover and bake about 30 minutes or until liquid is absorbed and juice of chicken is no longer pink when center of thickest part is cut (170°F).

1 Serving: Calories 340 (Calories from Fat 125); Total Fat 14g (Saturated Fat 7g); Cholesterol 105mg; Sodium 320mg; Total Carbohydrate 23g (Dietary Fiber 2g); Protein 32g

chicken-rice skillet

Prep Time: 15 min ∎ **Start to Finish:** 20 min ∎ 4 Servings

1 tablespoon vegetable oil

1¼ lb boneless skinless chicken breasts, cut into 1-inch pieces

2 cups water

1 tablespoon butter or margarine

1 bag (1 lb) frozen broccoli, red peppers, onions and mushrooms (or other combination), thawed, drained

2 cups uncooked instant rice

1 teaspoon salt

¼ teaspoon pepper

1 cup shredded Cheddar cheese (4 oz)

1 In 12-inch skillet, heat oil over medium-high heat. Cook chicken in oil 3 to 4 minutes, stirring occasionally, until no longer pink in center.

2 Add water and butter; heat to boiling. Stir in vegetables, rice, salt and pepper. Sprinkle with cheese; remove from heat.

3 Cover and let stand about 5 minutes or until water is absorbed.

1 Serving: Calories 580 (Calories from Fat 190); Total Fat 21g (Saturated Fat 9g); Cholesterol 125mg; Sodium 870mg; Total Carbohydrate 54g (Dietary Fiber 3g); Protein 45g

thai-style coconut chicken

Prep Time: 35 min ■ **Start to Finish:** 35 min ■ 4 Servings

1 tablespoon vegetable oil

1 lb boneless skinless chicken breasts, cut into bite-size pieces

1 teaspoon grated lime peel

1 teaspoon grated gingerroot

1 clove garlic, finely chopped

2 fresh serrano chiles or 1 jalapeño chile, seeded, finely chopped

¹/₄ cup finely chopped fresh cilantro

1 can (about 14 oz) coconut milk (not cream of coconut)

1 teaspoon packed brown sugar

¹/₂ teaspoon salt

1 tablespoon soy sauce

1 cup sugar snap peas

1 medium green bell pepper, cut into 1-inch squares

1 medium tomato, chopped (³/₄ cup)

1 tablespoon chopped fresh basil leaves

Hot cooked jasmine rice, if desired

1 In nonstick wok or 12-inch nonstick skillet, heat oil over high heat. Add chicken; stir-fry 2 to 3 minutes or until chicken is no longer pink in center. Add lime peel, gingerroot, garlic, chiles and cilantro; stir-fry 1 minute.

2 Pour coconut milk over chicken. Stir in brown sugar, salt, soy sauce, peas and bell pepper. Reduce heat to medium. Simmer uncovered 3 to 5 minutes, stirring occasionally, until vegetables are crisp-tender. Stir into tomato.

3 Spoon into 4 shallow serving bowls; top with basil. Serve with rice.

1 Serving: Calories 430 (Calories from Fat 230); Total Fat 26g (Saturated Fat 17g); Cholesterol 85mg; Sodium 650mg; Total Carbohydrate 14g (Dietary Fiber 4g); Protein 35g

Typical of many Thai dishes, the consistency of this recipe is like a broth, yet it's full of flavor. If you prefer your Thai food quite hot, increase the number of chiles.

6

fresh fish and seafood

salmon burgers with sour cream–dill sauce

Prep Time: 30 min ■ **Start to Finish:** 30 min ■ 4 Servings

Sour Cream–Dill Sauce
1/3 cup sour cream

3 tablespoons mayonnaise or salad dressing

3/4 teaspoon dried dill weed

Salmon Burgers
1 egg

2 tablespoons milk

1 can (14.75 oz) red or pink salmon, drained, skin
and bones removed and salmon flaked

2 medium green onions, chopped (2 tablespoons)

1 cup soft bread crumbs (about 1½ slices bread)

1/4 teaspoon salt

1 tablespoon vegetable oil

1 In small bowl, stir all sauce ingredients until well mixed; refrigerate until serving.

2 In medium bowl, beat egg and milk with fork or whisk. Stir in remaining ingredients except oil. Shape mixture into 4 patties, about 4 inches in diameter.

3 In 10-inch nonstick skillet, heat oil over medium heat. Cook patties in oil about 8 minutes, turning once, until golden brown. Serve with sauce.

1 Serving: Calories 300 (Calories from Fat 200); Total Fat 22g (Saturated Fat 6g); Cholesterol 120mg; Sodium 750mg; Total Carbohydrate 6g (Dietary Fiber 0g); Protein 20g

lemon and herb salmon packets

Prep Time: 30 min ▪ **Start to Finish:** 30 min ▪ 4 Servings

2 cups uncooked instant rice

1 can (14 oz) fat-free or low-sodium chicken broth

1 cup julienne (matchstick-cut) carrots (from 10-oz bag)

4 salmon fillets (4 to 6 oz each)

1 teaspoon lemon-pepper seasoning salt

$^1/_3$ cup chopped fresh chives

1 medium lemon, cut lengthwise in half, then cut crosswise into $^1/_4$-inch slices

1 Heat gas or charcoal grill for direct heat. Spray four 18×12-inch sheets of heavy-duty foil with cooking spray.

2 In medium bowl, mix rice and broth. Let stand about 5 minutes or until most of broth is absorbed. Stir in carrots.

3 Place salmon fillet on center of each foil sheet. Sprinkle with lemon pepper seasoning salt; top with chives. Arrange lemon slices over salmon. Spoon rice mixture around each fillet. Fold foil over salmon and rice so edges meet. Seal edges, making tight $^1/_2$-inch fold; fold again. Allow space on sides for circulation and expansion.

4 Cover and grill packets 4 to 6 inches from low heat 11 to 14 minutes or until salmon flakes easily with fork. Place packets on plates. Cut large X across top of each packet; carefully fold back foil to allow steam to escape.

1 Serving: Calories 400 (Calories from Fat 70); Total Fat 8g (Saturated Fat 2g); Cholesterol 75mg; Sodium 870mg; Total Carbohydrate 51g (Dietary Fiber 2g); Protein 31g

salmon with soy-ginger sauce

Prep Time: 25 min ■ Start to Finish: 25 min ■ 4 Servings

Salmon
2 tablespoons olive oil

4 salmon steaks, about $^3/_4$ inch thick (2 lb)

Soy-Ginger Sauce
$^1/_4$ cup plus 2 tablespoons soy sauce

$^1/_4$ cup mirin (sweet rice wine) or apple juice

2 tablespoons lime juice

2 tablespoons water

1 tablespoon honey

1 tablespoon grated gingerroot

1 In 10-inch skillet (preferably nonstick), heat oil over medium-high heat until shimmering and hot. Add salmon and cook 3 minutes or until brown on one side. Flip and brown other side, about 3 minutes longer.

2 In small bowl, mix all sauce ingredients. Add mixture to skillet. Reduce heat to medium-low.

3 Cover and cook 8 to 12 minutes or until salmon flakes easily with fork. Place salmon on serving plates and drizzle with sauce.

1 Serving: Calories 370 (Calories from Fat 160); Total Fat 18g (Saturated Fat 4g); Cholesterol 125mg; Sodium 1480mg; Total Carbohydrate 9g (Dietary Fiber 0g); Protein 42g

lemony fish over vegetables and rice

Prep Time: 30 min ▪ **Start to Finish:** 30 min ▪ 4 Servings

1 box (6 oz) fried rice (rice and vermicelli mix with almonds and Oriental seasonings)

2 tablespoons butter or margarine

2 cups water

$^1/_2$ teaspoon grated lemon peel

1 bag (1 lb) frozen broccoli, corn and peppers (or other combination)

1 lb cod, haddock or other mild-flavored fish fillets, about $^1/_2$ inch thick, cut into 4 serving pieces

$^1/_2$ teaspoon lemon-pepper seasoning

1 tablespoon lemon juice

Chopped fresh parsley, if desired

1 In 12-inch nonstick skillet, cook rice and butter over medium heat about 3 minutes, stirring occasionally, until rice is golden brown. Stir in water, seasoning packet from rice mix and lemon peel. Heat to boiling; reduce heat to low. Cover; simmer 10 minutes.

2 Stir in frozen vegetables. Heat to boiling over medium-high heat, stirring occasionally. Arrange fish on rice mixture. Sprinkle fish with lemon-pepper seasoning; drizzle with lemon juice.

3 Reduce heat to low. Cover; simmer 8 to 12 minutes or until fish flakes easily with fork and vegetables are tender. Sprinkle with parsley.

1 Serving: Calories 250 (Calories from Fat 70); Total Fat 8g (Saturated Fat 4g); Cholesterol 75mg; Sodium 620mg; Total Carbohydrate 19g (Dietary Fiber 3g); Protein 26g

graham-crusted tilapia

Prep Time: 15 min ▪ **Start to Finish:** 25 min ▪ 4 Servings

1 lb tilapia, cod, haddock or other medium-firm fish fillets, about $^3/_4$ inch thick

$^1/_2$ cup graham cracker crumbs (about 8 squares)

1 teaspoon grated lemon peel

$^1/_4$ teaspoon salt

$^1/_8$ teaspoon pepper

$^1/_4$ cup milk

2 tablespoons canola or soybean oil

2 tablespoons chopped toasted pecans*

1 Move oven rack to position slightly above middle of oven. Heat oven to 500°F.

2 Cut fish fillets crosswise into 2-inch-wide pieces. In shallow dish, mix cracker crumbs, lemon peel, salt and pepper. Place milk in another shallow dish.

3 Dip fish into milk, then coat with cracker mixture; place in ungreased 13×9-inch pan. Drizzle oil over fish; sprinkle with pecans.

4 Bake uncovered about 10 minutes or until fish flakes easily with fork.

*To toast nuts, bake uncovered in ungreased shallow pan in 350°F oven about 10 minutes, stirring occasionally, until golden brown.

1 Serving: Calories 230 (Calories from Fat 110); Total Fat 12g (Saturated Fat 1.5g); Cholesterol 60mg; Sodium 310mg; Total Carbohydrate 9g (Dietary Fiber 0g); Protein 23g

Here's a great new use for graham crackers!

gingered shrimp

Prep Time: 20 min ▪ **Start to Finish:** 2 hr 20 min ▪ 40 to 45 Shrimp

1¹/₂ lb cooked deveined peeled medium shrimp, thawed if frozen

¹/₄ cup soy sauce

2 teaspoons chopped gingerroot

¹/₄ cup white vinegar

2 tablespoons sugar

2 tablespoons sake or apple juice

1¹/₂ teaspoons salt

2 or 3 medium green onions, thinly sliced (2 to 3 tablespoons)

1 In 11×7-inch glass or plastic container, arrange shrimp in single layer. In 1-quart saucepan, heat soy sauce to boiling over high heat. Stir in gingerroot; reduce heat to medium. Simmer uncovered about 5 minutes or until liquid is reduced by half. Stir in vinegar, sugar, sake and salt; pour over shrimp. Cover; refrigerate 2 to 3 hours.

2 Remove shrimp from marinade with slotted spoon; arrange on serving plate. Discard marinade. Sprinkle onions over shrimp. Serve shrimp with toothpicks.

1 Shrimp: Calories 15 (Calories from Fat 0); Total Fat 0g (Saturated Fat 0g); Cholesterol 35mg; Sodium 85mg; Total Carbohydrate 0g (Dietary Fiber 0g); Protein 4g

Make it easy on your guests. Because these shrimp will be eaten with the fingers, purchase shrimp with the tail on for a prettier look. Provide a small bowl for the tails.

spicy lemon shrimp with basil mayonnaise

Prep Time: 15 min ■ **Start to Finish:** 15 min ■ About 24 Appetizers

1 tablespoon grated lemon peel

3 tablespoons lemon juice

³/₄ teaspoon crushed red pepper

¹/₂ teaspoon salt

2 cloves garlic, finely chopped

3 tablespoons olive or vegetable oil

1 lb uncooked peeled deveined large shrimp (21 to 30), thawed if frozen

¹/₂ cup loosely packed fresh basil leaves

¹/₂ cup mayonnaise or salad dressing

1 Set oven control to broil. In medium glass or plastic bowl, mix lemon peel, lemon juice, red pepper, salt, garlic and 1 tablespoon of the oil. Add shrimp; toss to coat. Spread shrimp in ungreased 15×10×1-inch pan. Broil with tops 2 to 3 inches from heat 3 to 5 minutes or until shrimp are pink.

2 In food processor, place basil and remaining 2 tablespoons oil. Cover and process until chopped. Add mayonnaise; cover and process until smooth. Serve shrimp with mayonnaise.

1 Appetizer: Calories 55 (Calories from Fat 45); Total Fat 5g (Saturated Fat 1g); Cholesterol 30mg; Sodium 95mg; Total Carbohydrate 0g (Dietary Fiber 0g); Protein 3g

shrimp creole

Prep Time: 1 hr ■ **Start to Finish:** 1 hr ■ 6 Servings

2 lb uncooked medium shrimp in shells, thawed if frozen

$^1/_4$ cup butter or margarine

3 medium onions, chopped (1$^1/_2$ cups)

2 medium green bell peppers, finely chopped (2 cups)

2 medium stalks celery, finely chopped (1 cup)

2 cloves garlic, finely chopped

1 cup water

2 teaspoons chopped fresh parsley

1$^1/_2$ teaspoons salt

$^1/_4$ teaspoon ground red pepper (cayenne)

2 dried bay leaves

1 can (15 oz) tomato sauce

6 cups hot cooked rice

1 Peel shrimp. Make a shallow cut lengthwise down back of each shrimp; wash out vein. Cover and refrigerate.

2 In 3-quart saucepan, melt butter over medium heat. Cook onions, bell peppers, celery and garlic in butter about 10 minutes, stirring occasionally, until onions are tender.

3 Stir in remaining ingredients except rice and shrimp. Heat to boiling; reduce heat to low. Simmer uncovered 10 minutes.

4 Stir in shrimp. Heat to boiling; reduce heat to medium. Cover and cook 4 to 6 minutes, stirring occasionally, until shrimp are pink. Remove bay leaves. Serve shrimp mixture over rice.

1 Serving: Calories 400 (Calories from Fat 80); Total Fat 9g (Saturated Fat 4.5g); Cholesterol 160mg; Sodium 1860mg; Total Carbohydrate 57g (Dietary Fiber 3g); Protein 22g

cioppino (italian seafood stew)

Prep Time: 20 min ∎ **Start to Finish:** 3 hrs 50 min ∎ 8 Servings

2 large onions, chopped (2 cups)

2 medium stalks celery, finely chopped (1 cup)

5 cloves garlic, finely chopped

1 can (28 oz) diced tomatoes, undrained

1 bottle (8 oz) clam juice

1 can (6 oz) tomato paste

$^1/_2$ cup dry white wine or water

1 tablespoon red wine vinegar

1 tablespoon olive or vegetable oil

$2^1/_2$ teaspoons Italian seasoning

$^1/_4$ teaspoon sugar

$^1/_4$ teaspoon crushed red pepper

1 dried bay leaf

1 lb firm-fleshed white fish, cut into 1-inch pieces

$^3/_4$ lb uncooked peeled deveined medium shrimp, thawed if frozen

1 can (6.5 oz) chopped clams with juice, undrained

1 can (6 oz) crabmeat, drained, cartilage removed and flaked

$^1/_4$ cup chopped fresh parsley

1 In 5- to 6-quart slow cooker, mix all ingredients except fish, shrimp, clams, crabmeat and parsley.

2 Cover and cook on high heat setting 3 to 4 hours or until vegetables are tender.

3 Stir in fish, shrimp, clams and crabmeat. Cover and cook on low heat setting 30 to 45 minutes or until fish flakes easily with fork. Remove bay leaf. Stir in parsley.

1 Serving: Calories 200 (Calories from Fat 35); Total Fat 4g (Saturated Fat 1g); Cholesterol 125mg; Sodium 600mg; Total Carbohydrate 15g (Dietary Fiber 3g); Protein 29g

scampi with fettuccine

Prep Time: 20 min ▪ **Start to Finish:** 20 min ▪ 4 Servings

8 oz uncooked regular or spinach fettuccine

2 tablespoons olive or vegetable oil

1¹/₂ lb uncooked deveined peeled medium shrimp, thawed if frozen, tail shells removed

2 medium green onions, thinly sliced (2 tablespoons)

2 cloves garlic, finely chopped

1 tablespoon chopped fresh or ¹/₂ teaspoon dried basil leaves

1 tablespoon chopped fresh parsley

2 tablespoons lemon juice

¹/₄ teaspoon salt

1 Cook and drain fettuccine as directed on package.

2 In 10-inch skillet, heat oil over medium heat. Cook remaining ingredients in oil 2 to 3 minutes, stirring frequently, until shrimp are pink; remove from heat.

3 Toss fettuccine with shrimp mixture in skillet.

1 Serving: Calories 380 (Calories from Fat 90); Total Fat 10g (Saturated Fat 1.5g); Cholesterol 290mg; Sodium 670mg; Total Carbohydrate 38g (Dietary Fiber 2g); Protein 33g

Peeling and deveining shrimp is time consuming—and unnecessary! Luckily for us, somebody else has done this laborious task. Look for fresh or frozen shrimp that have already been peeled and deveined and had their tail shells removed.

ramen shrimp and vegetables

Prep Time: 20 min ■ **Start to Finish:** 20 min ■ 4 Servings

1 lb uncooked peeled deveined medium shrimp, thawed if frozen, tail shells removed
2 cups water
1 package (3 oz) Oriental-flavor ramen noodle soup mix
1 bag (1 lb) fresh stir-fry vegetables
¼ cup stir-fry sauce

1 Heat 12-inch nonstick skillet over medium-high heat. Cook shrimp in skillet 2 to 4 minutes, stirring occasionally, until pink. Remove shrimp from skillet; keep warm.

2 In same skillet, heat water to boiling. Break up noodles from soup mix into water; stir until slightly softened. Stir in vegetables.

3 Heat to boiling. Boil 4 to 6 minutes, stirring occasionally, until vegetables are crisp-tender. Stir in seasoning packet from soup mix and stir-fry sauce. Cook 3 to 5 minutes, stirring frequently, until hot. Stir in shrimp.

1 Serving: Calories 210 (Calories from Fat 40); Total Fat 4.5g (Saturated Fat 1g); Cholesterol 160mg; Sodium 1160mg; Total Carbohydrate 21g (Dietary Fiber 3g); Protein 22g

Not in the mood for shrimp? Substitute 1 lb beef strips for stir-fry for the shrimp. Cook the beef in a heated skillet sprayed with cooking oil for 3 to 5 minutes, stirring occasionally, until no longer pink.

linguine with red clam sauce

Prep Time: 40 min ▪ **Start to Finish:** 1 hr ▪ 6 Servings

Red Clam Sauce
1 pint shucked fresh small clams, drained,
   liquor reserved*
¼ cup olive or vegetable oil
3 cloves garlic, finely chopped
1 can (28 oz) Italian-style (plum) tomatoes, drained
   and chopped
1 small jalapeño chile, seeded, finely chopped
1 tablespoon chopped fresh parsley
1 teaspoon salt

Linguine
8 oz uncooked linguine

Garnish
Chopped fresh parsley

1 Chop clams; set aside. In 3-quart saucepan, heat oil over medium-high heat. Cook garlic in oil, stirring frequently, until golden. Stir in tomatoes and chile. Cook 3 minutes, stirring frequently. Stir in clam liquor. Heat to boiling; reduce heat. Simmer uncovered 10 minutes. Stir in clams, parsley and salt. Cover and simmer about 15 minutes, stirring occasionally, until clams are tender.

2 Meanwhile, cook and drain linguine as directed on package. Keep warm.

3 In large bowl, toss linguine and sauce. Sprinkle with parsley.

*2 cans (6.5 oz each) minced clams, undrained, can be substituted for the fresh clams. Decrease simmer time to 5 minutes.

1 Serving: Calories 300 (Calories from Fat 90); Total Fat 10g (Saturated Fat 1.5g); Cholesterol 15mg; Sodium 620mg; Total Carbohydrate 38g (Dietary Fiber 4g); Protein 13g

7

**great for
the grill**

grilled potato wedges with barbecue dipping sauce

Prep Time: 45 min ■ **Start to Finish:** 45 min ■ 4 Servings

4 medium white potatoes
Cooking spray
1 teaspoon Cajun seasoning
$^1/_2$ cup reduced-fat sour cream
2 tablespoons barbecue sauce

1 Heat gas or charcoal grill for direct heat. Cut each potato lengthwise into 8 wedges; pat dry with paper towels. Spray potato wedges thoroughly with cooking spray. Sprinkle with Cajun seasoning. Place in grill basket (grill "wok").

2 Cover and grill potato wedges over medium heat 30 to 40 minutes, stirring every 10 minutes, until tender.

3 In small bowl, mix sour cream and barbecue sauce. Serve with potato wedges.

1 Serving: Calories 160 (Calories from Fat 40); Total Fat 4g (Saturated Fat 2.5g); Cholesterol 10mg; Sodium 240mg; Total Carbohydrate 30g (Dietary Fiber 3g); Protein 4g

If Cajun seasoning isn't available, make your own seasoning, using $^1/_2$ teaspoon chili powder, $^1/_4$ teaspoon ground oregano and $^1/_4$ teaspoon onion or garlic salt.

portabella mushrooms with herbs

Prep Time: 20 min ▪ **Start to Finish:** 1 hr 30 min ▪ 4 Servings

2 tablespoons olive or vegetable oil

1 tablespoon balsamic vinegar

1 teaspoon chopped fresh or $1/4$ teaspoon dried oregano leaves

1 teaspoon chopped fresh or $1/4$ teaspoon dried thyme leaves

$1/8$ teaspoon salt

1 clove garlic, finely chopped

4 fresh portabella mushroom caps (about 4 inches in diameter)

$1/4$ cup crumbled feta cheese with herbs

1 In large glass or plastic bowl or resealable food-storage plastic bag, mix oil, vinegar, oregano, thyme, salt and garlic. Add mushrooms; turn to coat. Cover dish or seal bag and refrigerate 1 hour.

2 Heat gas or charcoal grill for direct heat. Remove mushrooms from marinade (mushrooms will absorb most of the marinade). Cover and grill mushrooms over medium heat 8 to 10 minutes or until tender. Sprinkle with cheese.

1 Serving: Calories 110 (Calories from Fat 80); Total Fat 9g (Saturated Fat 2.5g); Cholesterol 10mg; Sodium 180mg; Total Carbohydrate 4g (Dietary Fiber 0g); Protein 3g

This is a great side dish to serve with almost any grilled meat. Or serve it as a first course.

vegetable kabobs with mustard dip

Prep Time: 35 min ■ **Start to Finish:** 1 hr 35 min ■ 9 Servings

Dip

¹/₂ cup sour cream

¹/₂ cup plain yogurt

1 tablespoon finely chopped fresh parsley

1 teaspoon onion powder

1 teaspoon garlic salt

1 tablespoon Dijon mustard

Kabobs

1 medium bell pepper, cut into 6 strips, then cut into thirds (18 pieces)

1 medium zucchini, cut diagonally into ¹/₂-inch slices

8 oz fresh whole mushrooms

9 large cherry tomatoes

2 tablespoons olive or vegetable oil

1 In small bowl, mix all dip ingredients. Cover; refrigerate at least 1 hour.

2 Heat gas or charcoal grill. On 5 (12-inch) metal skewers, thread vegetables so that one kind of vegetable is on the same skewer (use 2 skewers for mushrooms); leave space between each piece. Brush vegetables with oil.

3 Place skewers of bell pepper and zucchini on grill. Cover grill; cook over medium heat 2 minutes. Add skewers of mushrooms and tomatoes. Cover grill; cook 4 to 5 minutes, carefully turning every 2 minutes, until vegetables are tender. Remove vegetables from skewers to serving plate. Serve with dip.

1 Serving: Calories 80 (Calories from Fat 50); Total Fat 6g (Saturated Fat 2g); Cholesterol 10mg; Sodium 170mg; Total Carbohydrate 5g (Dietary Fiber 1g); Protein 2g

Choose red bell peppers for beautiful color and a sweeter flavor than green bell pepper.

lemon-pesto shrimp and scallops

Prep Time: 25 min ▮ **Start to Finish:** 25 min ▮ 6 Servings

1 lb uncooked peeled deveined large shrimp, thawed if frozen and tails peeled

1 lb uncooked sea scallops

¼ cup refrigerated basil pesto (from 7-oz container)

1 teaspoon grated lemon peel

¼ teaspoon salt

¼ teaspoon coarse ground pepper

1 Heat coals or gas grill for direct heat. In large bowl, mix all ingredients. Place seafood mixture in grill basket (grill "wok").

2 Cover and grill seafood mixture over medium heat 10 to 12 minutes, shaking basket or stirring seafood mixture occasionally, until shrimp are pink and firm and scallops are white.

1 Serving: Calories 150 (Calories from Fat 60); Total Fat 7g (Saturated Fat 1.5g); Cholesterol 130mg; Sodium 410mg; Total Carbohydrate 0g (Dietary Fiber 0g); Protein 21g

If you don't have a grill basket, double a sheet of heavy-duty foil and poke several holes in it. Then grill this dish according to the recipe.

surf and turf kabobs

Prep Time: 15 min ∎ **Start to Finish:** 50 min ∎ 12 Kabobs

³/₄ lb boneless beef sirloin (³/₄ inch thick), trimmed of fat
12 uncooked peeled deveined medium or large shrimp, thawed if frozen and tails removed
¹/₂ cup teriyaki marinade and sauce (from 10-oz bottle)
¹/₄ teaspoon coarsely ground pepper

1 Cut beef into 24 (1-inch) pieces. In medium bowl, mix beef, shrimp and teriyaki sauce. Sprinkle with pepper. Cover and refrigerate 30 minutes, stirring frequently, to marinate. Meanwhile, soak twelve 4- to 6-inch wooden skewers in water 30 minutes to prevent burning.

2 Spray broiler pan rack with cooking spray. On each skewer, thread 1 beef piece, 1 shrimp and another beef piece, reserving marinade. Place kabobs on rack in broiler pan.

3 Broil kabobs with tops 4 to 6 inches from heat 5 to 6 minutes, turning once and basting with marinade once or twice, until shrimp are pink. Discard any remaining marinade.

1 Kabob: Calories 40 (Calories from Fat 10); Total Fat 1g (Saturated Fat 0g); Cholesterol 25mg; Sodium 330mg; Total Carbohydrate 1g (Dietary Fiber 0g); Protein 7g

For fun, you can also serve these meat and seafood kabobs with a variety of sauces. Try small bowls of sweet-and-sour sauce and horseradish-mustard sauce.

ginger-lime tuna steaks

Prep Time: 25 min ▪ **Start to Finish:** 1 hr 25 min ▪ 4 Servings

1½ lb tuna steaks, ¾ to 1 inch thick

¼ cup lime juice

2 tablespoons olive or vegetable oil

2 teaspoons finely chopped gingerroot

½ teaspoon salt

⅛ teaspoon ground red pepper (cayenne)

2 cloves garlic, crushed

Lime wedges, if desired

1 If fish steaks are large, cut into 6 serving pieces. In shallow glass or plastic dish or resealable food-storage plastic bag, mix remaining ingredients except lime wedges. Add fish; turn to coat. Cover dish or seal bag and refrigerate, turning fish once, at least 1 hour but no longer than 24 hours.

2 Heat gas or charcoal grill for direct heat. Remove fish from marinade; reserve marinade. Cover and grill fish about 4 inches from medium heat 11 to 15 minutes, brushing 2 or 3 times with marinade and turning once, until fish flakes easily with fork and is slightly pink in center. Discard any remaining marinade. Serve fish with lime wedges.

1 Serving: Calories 280 (Calories from Fat 120); Total Fat 13g (Saturated Fat 3g); Cholesterol 65mg; Sodium 270mg; Total Carbohydrate 0g (Dietary Fiber 0g); Protein 40g

For variety, try using swordfish or halibut steaks instead of the tuna steaks.

mediterranean chicken vegetable kabobs

Prep Time: 25 min ■ **Start to Finish:** 55 min ■ 4 Kabobs

Rosemary Lemon Marinade

$1/4$ cup lemon juice

3 tablespoons olive or vegetable oil

2 teaspoons chopped fresh or 1 teaspoon dried
rosemary leaves

$1/2$ teaspoon salt

$1/4$ teaspoon pepper

4 cloves garlic, finely chopped

Chicken Kabobs

1 lb boneless skinless chicken breasts, cut into
$1^1/2$-inch pieces

1 medium red bell pepper, cut into 1-inch pieces

1 medium zucchini or yellow summer squash, cut
into 1-inch pieces

1 medium red onion, cut into wedges

1 lb asparagus spears

$1/4$ cup feta cheese

1 In shallow glass or plastic dish, mix all marinade ingredients. Add chicken; stir to coat. Cover dish and refrigerate, stirring chicken occasionally, at least 30 minutes but no longer than 6 hours.

2 Heat gas or charcoal grill for direct heat. Remove chicken from marinade; reserve marinade. Thread chicken, bell pepper, zucchini and onion alternately on each of four 15-inch metal skewers, leaving space between each piece. Brush vegetables with marinade.

3 Cover and grill kabobs 4 to 6 inches from medium heat 10 to 15 minutes, turning and brushing frequently with marinade, until chicken is no longer pink in center. Add asparagus to grill for last 5 minutes, turning occasionally, until crisp-tender. Discard any remaining marinade.

4 Sprinkle cheese over kabobs and serve with asparagus.

1 Kabob: Calories 260 (Calories from Fat 115): Total Fat 13g (Saturated Fat 3g); Cholesterol 75mg; Sodium 370mg; Total Carbohydrate 10g (Dietary Fiber 3g); Protein 29g

For a great side dish toss cooked rosamarina (orzo) pasta with chopped fresh herbs. Thyme and Italian parsley are terrific.

buffalo chicken kabobs

Prep Time: 40 min ▪ **Start to Finish:** 40 min ▪ 4 Servings

1 lb boneless skinless chicken breasts, cut into 24 cubes

24 (about 1¹/₂ cups) refrigerated new potato wedges (from 1-lb 4-oz bag)

24 pieces (about 1 inch) celery

2 tablespoons olive or vegetable oil

1 teaspoon red pepper sauce

¹/₂ teaspoon black and red pepper blend

¹/₂ teaspoon seasoned salt

6 cups torn romaine lettuce

¹/₂ cup shredded carrot

¹/₂ cup blue cheese dressing

1 Heat gas or charcoal grill for direct heat. On each of eight 8- to 10-inch metal skewers, thread chicken, potatoes and celery alternately, leaving ¹/₄-inch space between each piece. In small bowl, mix oil and pepper sauce; brush over chicken and vegetables. Sprinkle with pepper blend and seasoned salt.

2 Cover and grill kabobs 4 to 6 inches from medium heat 15 to 20 minutes, turning occasionally, until chicken is no longer pink in center and potatoes are tender.

3 Arrange romaine and carrot on 4 individual serving plates. Top each with 2 kabobs. Serve with dressing.

1 Serving (2 Kabobs): Calories 430 (Calories from Fat 210); Total Fat 24g (Saturated Fat 3g); Cholesterol 75mg; Sodium 590mg; Total Carbohydrate 26g (Dietary Fiber 5g); Protein 29g

This is a super one-dish entrée salad, so all you need to add is warm garlic bread. Wrap the bread in foil, then heat it on the grill for 5 to 10 minutes.

grilled chicken with chipotle-peach glaze

Prep Time: 30 min ∎ **Start to Finish:** 30 min ∎ 8 Servings

$^1/_2$ **cup peach preserves**

$^1/_4$ **cup lime juice**

1 chipotle chile in adobo sauce (from 7-oz can), seeded, chopped

1 teaspoon adobo sauce (from can of chiles)

2 tablespoons chopped fresh cilantro

1 teaspoon garlic-pepper blend

$^1/_2$ **teaspoon ground cumin**

$^1/_2$ **teaspoon salt**

8 boneless skinless chicken breasts (about 2$^1/_2$ lb)

4 ripe peaches, cut in half, pitted

Cilantro sprigs, if desired

1 Heat gas or charcoal grill.

2 In 1-quart saucepan, mix preserves, lime juice, chile and adobo sauce. Heat over low heat, stirring occasionally, until preserves are melted. Stir in chopped cilantro; set aside.

3 In small bowl, mix garlic-pepper, cumin and salt. Sprinkle both sides of chicken with mixture.

4 Cover and grill chicken on medium heat 15 to 20 minutes, turning once or twice and brushing with preserves mixture during last 2 minutes of grilling, until juice of chicken is clear when center of thickest part is cut. Add peach halves to grill for last 2 to 3 minutes of grilling just until heated.

5 In 1-quart saucepan, heat any remaining preserves mixture to boiling; boil and stir 1 minute. Serve with chicken and peaches. Garnish with cilantro sprigs.

1 Serving: Calories 250 (Calories from Fat 45); Total Fat 5g (Saturated Fat 1.5g); Cholesterol 85mg; Sodium 270mg; Total Carbohydrate 20g (Dietary Fiber 2g); Protein 32g

When working with canned chipotle in adobo, use caution and rubber gloves.

grilled pesto chicken packets

Prep Time: 40 min ■ **Start to Finish:** 40 min ■ 4 Packets

4 boneless skinless chicken breasts (about 1¹/₄ lb)
8 plum (Roma) tomatoes, cut into ¹/₂-inch slices
4 small zucchini, cut into ¹/₂-inch slices
¹/₂ cup basil pesto

1 Heat gas or charcoal grill for direct heat. Place 1 chicken breast, 2 sliced tomatoes and 1 sliced zucchini on one side of four 18×12-inch sheets of heavy-duty foil. Spoon 2 tablespoons pesto over chicken mixture on each sheet.

2 Fold foil over chicken and vegetables so edges meet. Seal edges, making tight ¹/₂-inch fold; fold again. Allow space on sides for circulation and expansion.

3 Cover and grill packets 4 to 5 inches from medium heat 20 to 25 minutes or until juice of chicken is no longer pink when center of thickest part is cut (170°F). Place packets on plates. Cut large X across top of packet; carefully fold back foil to allow steam to escape.

1 Packet: Calories 330 (Calories from Fat 180); Total Fat 20g (Saturated Fat 4g); Cholesterol 80mg; Sodium 350mg; Total Carbohydrate 10g (Dietary Fiber 3g); Protein 31g

chicken with oregano-peach sauce

Prep Time: 35 min ▪ **Start to Finish:** 35 min ▪ 4 Servings

$1/2$ **cup peach preserves**

$1/4$ **cup raspberry vinegar**

2 tablespoons chopped fresh oregano leaves

4 boneless skinless chicken breasts (about $1^1/4$ lb)

$1/2$ **teaspoon garlic-pepper blend**

$1/2$ **teaspoon seasoned salt**

1 Heat gas or charcoal grill for direct heat. In 1-quart saucepan, heat preserves and vinegar to boiling, stirring constantly, until preserves are melted. Spoon about $1/4$ cup mixture into small bowl or custard cup for brushing on chicken. Stir oregano into remaining mixture and reserve to serve with chicken.

2 Sprinkle chicken with garlic-pepper blend and seasoned salt.

3 Cover and grill chicken 4 to 6 inches from medium heat 15 to 20 minutes, turning once and brushing with preserves mixture during last 10 minutes of grilling, until juice of chicken is no longer pink when center of thickest part is cut (170°F). Discard any remaining preserves mixture brushed on chicken. Serve chicken with reserved preserves mixture with oregano.

1 Serving: Calories 220 (Calories from Fat 35); Total Fat 4g (Saturated Fat 1g); Cholesterol 75mg; Sodium 250mg; Total Carbohydrate 19g (Dietary Fiber 0g); Protein 27g

When buying fresh oregano, look for bright-green bunches with no sign of wilting or yellowing. Store it in the refrigerator in a plastic bag for up to 3 days.

barbecue pork bites

Prep Time: 35 min ∎ **Start to Finish:** 50 min ∎ 8 Servings

1 pork tenderloin ($^3/_4$ to 1 lb)
1 tablespoon chili powder
1 teaspoon ground cumin
1 teaspoon packed brown sugar
$^1/_4$ teaspoon garlic powder
$^1/_8$ teaspoon ground red pepper (cayenne)
$^1/_2$ cup mayonnaise or salad dressing
$^1/_2$ teaspoon ground mustard
1 medium green onion, finely chopped (1 tablespoon)

1 Cut pork into 32 (1-inch) pieces; place in medium bowl. In small bowl, mix chili powder, cumin, brown sugar, garlic powder and red pepper. Reserve 2 teaspoons spice mixture; sprinkle remaining mixture over pork pieces; stir to coat completely. Let stand 15 minutes.

2 In small bowl, mix mayonnaise, mustard, reserved 2 teaspoons spice mixture and the onion; set aside.

3 Heat gas or charcoal grill. Spray grill basket (grill "wok") with cooking spray. Spoon pork into basket.

4 Place basket on grill. Cover grill; cook over medium heat 10 to 12 minutes, shaking basket or stirring pork once or twice, until pork is no longer pink in center. Serve with toothpicks and mayonnaise mixture for dipping.

To broil pork: Set oven control to broil. Spray rack of broiler pan with cooking spray. Place pork on rack. Broil with tops 6 inches from heat about 10 minutes, turning once, until no longer pink in center.

1 Serving (4 pork pieces): Calories 160 (Calories from Fat 110); Total Fat 13g (Saturated Fat 2g); Cholesterol 30mg; Sodium 105mg; Total Carbohydrate 2g (Dietary Fiber 0g); Protein 10g

Great For the Grill **245**

italian sausage burgers

Prep Time: 25 min ∎ **Start to Finish:** 25 min ∎ 6 Sandwiches

1 lb lean (at least 80%) ground beef
$^1/_2$ lb bulk mild or hot Italian sausage
2 tablespoons Italian-style dry bread crumbs
6 slices ($^3/_4$ oz each) mozzarella cheese
12 slices Italian bread, $^1/_2$ inch thick
$^1/_2$ cup sun-dried tomato mayonnaise
1 cup shredded lettuce
1 medium tomato, thinly sliced

1 Heat gas or charcoal grill for direct heat. In large bowl, mix beef, sausage and bread crumbs. Shape mixture into 6 patties, about $^1/_2$ inch thick and $3^1/_2$ inches in diameter.

2 Cover and grill patties 4 to 6 inches from medium heat 12 to 15 minutes, turning once, until meat thermometer inserted in center reads 160°F. Top patties with cheese. Cover and grill about 1 minute longer or until cheese is melted. Add bread slices to side of grill for last 2 to 3 minutes of grilling, turning once, until lightly toasted.

3 Spread toasted bread with mayonnaise; top 6 bread slices with lettuce, tomato and patties. Top with remaining bread slices.

1 Sandwich: Calories 490 (Calories from Fat 280); Total Fat 31g (Saturated Fat 10g); Cholesterol 85mg; Sodium 750mg; Total Carbohydrate 25g (Dietary Fiber 2g); Protein 29g

You can make your own sun-dried tomato mayonnaise by combining $^1/_3$ cup mayonnaise with about 2 tablespoons chopped sun-dried tomatoes. Plain mayonnaise works fine here, too.

chipotle salsa ribs

Prep Time: 10 min ▪ **Start to Finish:** 6 hrs 10 min ▪ 6 Servings

Southwestern Rub

1 tablespoon packed brown sugar

1 teaspoon chili powder

1 teaspoon paprika

$^1/_2$ teaspoon ground cumin

$^1/_2$ teaspoon seasoned salt

$^1/_2$ teaspoon garlic-pepper blend

$^1/_4$ teaspoon ground ginger

Ribs

4 lb pork loin back ribs (not cut into serving pieces)

$^1/_2$ cup chipotle salsa

$^1/_4$ cup chili sauce

2 tablespoons orange marmalade

1 In small bowl, mix all rub ingredients. Rub mixture over ribs. Wrap tightly in plastic wrap and refrigerate at least 4 hours but no longer than 12 hours.

2 If using charcoal grill, place drip pan directly under grilling area, and arrange coals around edge of firebox. Heat gas or charcoal grill for indirect heat. Cover and grill ribs over drip pan or over unheated side of gas grill and 4 to 6 inches from medium heat 1 hour 30 minutes to 2 hours, turning occasionally, until tender.

3 In small bowl, mix salsa, chili sauce and marmalade. Brush over ribs during last 10 to 15 minutes of grilling. Heat remaining salsa mixture to boiling; boil and stir 1 minute. Cut ribs into serving-size pieces. Serve salsa mixture with ribs.

1 Serving: Calories 610 (Calories from Fat 400); Total Fat 44g (Saturated Fat 16g); Cholesterol 175mg; Sodium 500mg; Total Carbohydrate 11g (Dietary Fiber 1g); Protein 43g

When food is cooked away from the heat source, it's called "indirect-heat" grilling. This is the best way to cook large cuts or long-cooking foods because the indirect heat won't burn or overcook the food.

jamaican jerk pork chops with mango salsa

Prep Time: 30 min ▪ **Start to Finish:** 1 hr ▪ 4 Servings

Jamaican Jerk Seasoning

2 teaspoons dried thyme leaves

1 teaspoon ground allspice

1 teaspoon brown sugar

$^1/_2$ teaspoon salt

$^1/_2$ teaspoon cracked black pepper

$^1/_4$ to $^1/_2$ teaspoon ground red pepper (cayenne)

$^1/_4$ teaspoon crushed dried sage leaves

4 cloves garlic, finely chopped

Pork Chops

4 pork loin or rib chops, about $^3/_4$ inch thick
   (about 2 lb)

Mango Salsa

1 medium mango, cut lengthwise in half, seed
   removed and chopped (1 cup)

$^1/_4$ cup finely chopped red onion

1 tablespoon finely chopped fresh or 1 teaspoon
   dried mint leaves

1 small jalapeño chile, finely chopped
   (2 to 3 teaspoons)

2 tablespoons lime juice

$^1/_8$ teaspoon salt

1 In small bowl, mix all seasoning ingredients. Rub seasoning into pork chops. Cover and refrigerate at least 30 minutes but no longer than 1 hour.

2 Meanwhile, in small glass or plastic bowl, mix all salsa ingredients. Cover and refrigerate until serving.

3 Heat gas or charcoal grill for direct heat.

4 Cover and grill pork chops over medium heat 9 to 12 minutes, turning once, until no longer pink and meat thermometer inserted in center reads 160°F. Serve with salsa.

1 Serving: Calories 215 (Calories from Fat 70); Total Fat 8g (Saturated Fat 3g); Cholesterol 65mg; Sodium 410mg; Total Carbohydrate 14g (Dietary Fiber 2g); Protein 24g

Instead of making your own jerk seasoning, use 2 tablespoons of purchased Jamaican jerk blend seasoning. You'll find it in the spice aisle of your supermarket.

grilled veggies and steak

Prep Time: 20 min ■ **Start to Finish:** 30 min ■ 4 Servings

1 package (6 oz) small fresh portabella mushrooms

$^1/_2$ lb beef sirloin steak (about $^3/_4$ inch thick), cut into $^3/_4$-inch cubes

1 cup frozen pearl onions (from 1-lb bag), thawed

$^1/_2$ cup plus 2 tablespoons balsamic vinaigrette

$^1/_2$ cup halved grape or cherry tomatoes

1 Heat gas or charcoal grill. In large bowl, place mushrooms, beef, onions and $^1/_2$ cup of the vinaigrette; toss to coat. Let stand 10 minutes; drain. Place mixture in grill basket (grill "wok"). Place basket on cookie sheet to carry to grill to catch drips.

2 Place basket on grill. Cover grill; cook over medium-high heat 7 to 9 minutes, shaking basket or stirring beef mixture twice, until vegetables are tender and beef is desired doneness. Stir in tomatoes.

3 Spoon beef mixture into serving dish. Stir in remaining 2 tablespoons vinaigrette.

1 Serving: Calories 150 (Calories from Fat 45); Total Fat 5g (Saturated Fat 1g); Cholesterol 30mg; Sodium 350mg; Total Carbohydrate 10g (Dietary Fiber 1g); Protein 15g

onion-topped caesar burgers

Prep Time: 30 min ▪ **Start to Finish:** 30 min ▪ 4 Sandwiches

1 lb lean (at least 80%) ground beef
2 tablespoons chopped fresh parsley
$^1/_2$ cup Caesar dressing
$^1/_2$ teaspoon peppered seasoned salt
1 small sweet onion (such as Bermuda, Maui, Spanish or
    Walla Walla), cut into $^1/_4$- to $^1/_2$-inch slices
$1^1/_2$ cups shredded romaine lettuce
2 tablespoons freshly shredded Parmesan cheese
4 sandwich buns, split

1 Heat gas or charcoal grill for direct heat. In medium bowl, mix beef, parsley, 2 tablespoons of the dressing and the peppered seasoned salt. Shape mixture into 4 patties, about $^1/_2$ inch thick.

2 Cover and grill patties over medium heat 10 to 12 minutes, turning once, until meat thermometer inserted in center reads 160°F. Add onion slices for last 8 to 10 minutes of grilling, brushing with 2 tablespoons of the dressing and turning once, until crisp-tender.

3 In small bowl, toss romaine, remaining $^1/_4$ cup dressing and the cheese. Layer romaine, burger and onion on bottom of each bun. Top with tops of buns.

1 Sandwich: Calories 500 (Calories from Fat 300); Total Fat 33g (Saturated Fat 9g); Cholesterol 75mg; Sodium 840mg; Total Carbohydrate 25g (Dietary Fiber 2g); Protein 26g

comfort classics

chicken pot pie

Prep Time: 15 min ■ **Start to Finish:** 45 min ■ 10 Servings

2 cans (10.75 oz each) condensed cream of chicken and mushroom soup
1 can (10.75 oz) condensed chicken broth
4 cups cut-up cooked chicken
1 bag (1 lb) frozen mixed vegetables, thawed, drained
2 cups Original Bisquick mix
1¹/₂ cups milk
¹/₂ teaspoon poultry seasoning

1 Heat oven to 375°F (350°F for glass baking dish). In 3-quart saucepan, heat soup, broth, chicken and vegetables to boiling, stirring constantly. Boil and stir 1 minute. Spread in ungreased 13×9-inch pan.

2 In medium bowl, stir together remaining ingredients. Pour over chicken mixture.

3 Bake uncovered about 30 minutes or until light brown.

1 Serving: Calories 285 (Calories from Fat 110); Total Fat 12g (Saturated Fat 4g); Cholesterol 55mg; Sodium 1040mg; Total Carbohydrate 24g (Dietary Fiber 2g); Protein 22g

It's hard to believe that comfort food could be so easy—it's homemade heaven!

mustardy chicken and dumplings

Prep Time: 35 min ▪ **Start to Finish:** 35 min ▪ 6 Servings

1 tablespoon vegetable oil

4 boneless skinless chicken breasts (about 1¼ lb), cut into bite-size pieces

1 medium onion, chopped (½ cup)

2 cups milk

2 cups frozen mixed vegetables

1 can (10.75 oz) condensed cream of chicken soup

1 tablespoon yellow mustard

1½ cups Original Bisquick mix

1 In 4-quart Dutch oven, heat oil over medium-high heat. Add chicken and onion; cook 6 to 8 minutes, stirring occasionally, until chicken is no longer pink in center and onion is tender.

2 Stir in 1½ cups of the milk, the mixed vegetables, soup and mustard. Heat to boiling.

3 In small bowl, stir Bisquick mix and remaining ½ cup milk until soft dough forms. Drop dough by 6 spoonfuls onto chicken mixture; reduce heat to low. Cover; cook 20 minutes.

1 Serving: Calories 390 (Calories from Fat 130); Total Fat 15g (Saturated Fat 4g); Cholesterol 65mg; Sodium 930mg; Total Carbohydrate 36g (Dietary Fiber 3g); Protein 29g

southern turkey and lentil casserole

Prep Time: 30 min ■ **Start to Finish:** 1 hr 40 min ■ 5 Servings

4 slices bacon, cut into ¹/₂-inch pieces
2 medium carrots, chopped (1 cup)
1 medium onion, chopped (¹/₂ cup)
1 cup dried lentils (8 oz), sorted, rinsed
1 can (15 to 16 oz) black-eyed peas, drained, rinsed
1 can (14.5 oz) stewed tomatoes with garlic, oregano and basil, undrained
1 can (14.5 oz) chicken broth
1¹/₂ cups ¹/₂-inch cubes cooked turkey or chicken
2 tablespoons chili sauce
Chopped fresh parsley, if desired

1 Heat oven to 350°F. Spray 13×9-inch (3-quart) glass baking dish with cooking spray.

2 In 10-inch nonstick skillet, cook bacon, carrots and onion over medium heat 3 to 5 minutes, stirring occasionally, until vegetables are crisp-tender. Stir in lentils. Cook 3 minutes, stirring occasionally.

3 Spoon mixture into baking dish. Stir in black-eyed peas, tomatoes, broth, turkey and chili sauce.

4 Cover and bake 60 to 70 minutes or until liquid is absorbed. Sprinkle with parsley.

1 Serving: Calories 330 (Calories from Fat 65); Total Fat 7g (Saturated Fat 2g); Cholesterol 40mg; Sodium 990mg; Total Carbohydrate 51g (Dietary Fiber 16g); Protein 32g

You can use ketchup in place of the chili sauce in this delicious casserole.

caribbean turkey stew

Prep Time: 40 min ▪ **Start to Finish:** 40 min ▪ 5 Servings

1 tablespoon olive or vegetable oil

1 medium onion, coarsely chopped (^{1}/$_2$ cup)

2 teaspoons finely chopped garlic

1^1/$_2$ lb turkey breast tenderloins, cut into 1-inch pieces

^{1}/$_2$ teaspoon salt

^{1}/$_2$ teaspoon ground nutmeg

^{1}/$_4$ teaspoon pepper

1 dark-orange sweet potato, peeled, cut into 1-inch pieces (1^1/$_2$ cups)

2 dried bay leaves

4 small red potatoes, cut into eighths (1^1/$_2$ cups)

2 cups chicken broth

2 cups frozen sweet peas (from 1-lb bag)

1. In 4^1/$_2$-quart Dutch oven, heat oil over medium-high heat. Cook onion and garlic in oil 4 to 5 minutes, stirring frequently, until onion is softened.

2. Sprinkle turkey pieces with salt, nutmeg and pepper. Stir into onion mixture. Cook 5 to 6 minutes, stirring occasionally, until turkey is no longer pink in center.

3. Stir in remaining ingredients except peas. Heat to boiling; reduce heat to medium-low. Cover and cook 18 to 20 minutes or until potatoes are tender.

4. Stir in peas. Cover and cook 4 to 5 minutes, stirring occasionally, until peas are hot. Remove bay leaves.

1 Serving: Calories 320 (Calories from Fat 45); Total Fat 5g (Saturated Fat 1g); Cholesterol 90mg; Sodium 760mg; Total Carbohydrate 34g (Dietary Fiber 6g); Protein 39g

A tropical salad of mango, papaya and bananas drizzled with fresh lime juice adds to the Caribbean flavor of this sweet and spicy stew.

turkey and cornbread casserole

Prep Time: 25 min ■ **Start to Finish:** 1 hr 40 min ■ 6 Servings

2 tablespoons butter or margarine
1 medium onion, chopped (¹/₂ cup)
1 small red bell pepper, chopped (¹/₂ cup)
4 cups seasoned cornbread stuffing mix
1 cup frozen whole kernel corn (from 1-lb bag)
1¹/₂ cups water
2 turkey breast tenderloins (about ³/₄ lb each)
¹/₂ teaspoon chili powder
¹/₂ teaspoon peppered seasoned salt

1 Heat oven to 350°F. Spray 11×7-inch (2-quart) glass baking dish with cooking spray. In 12-inch nonstick skillet, melt butter over medium-high heat. Cook onion and bell pepper in butter 2 to 3 minutes, stirring frequently, until tender. Stir in stuffing mix, corn and water. Spread stuffing mixture in baking dish.

2 Sprinkle both sides of turkey tenderloins with chili powder and peppered seasoned salt. Place on stuffing, pressing into stuffing mixture slightly. Spray sheet of foil with cooking spray. Cover baking dish with foil, sprayed side down.

3 Bake 1 hour. Uncover and bake 10 to 15 minutes longer or until juice of turkey is clear when center of thickest part is cut to bone.

1 Serving: Calories 330 (Calories from Fat 60); Total Fat 7g (Saturated Fat 2.5g); Cholesterol 85mg; Sodium 620mg; Total Carbohydrate 37g (Dietary Fiber 3g); Protein 31g

winter vegetable stew

Prep Time: 20 min ▪ **Start to Finish:** 8 hr 40 min ▪ 8 Servings

1 can (28 oz) Italian-style peeled whole tomatoes
4 medium red potatoes, cut into $^1/_2$-inch pieces
4 medium stalks celery, cut into $^1/_2$-inch pieces (2 cups)
3 medium carrots, cut into $^1/_2$-inch pieces (1$^1/_2$ cups)
2 medium parsnips, peeled, cut into $^1/_2$-inch pieces
2 medium leeks, cut into $^1/_2$-inch pieces
1 can (14 oz) chicken broth
$^1/_2$ teaspoon dried thyme leaves
$^1/_2$ teaspoon dried rosemary leaves
$^1/_2$ teaspoon salt
3 tablespoons cornstarch
3 tablespoons cold water

1 Drain tomatoes, reserving liquid. Cut tomatoes into $^1/_2$-inch pieces. In 4- to 5-quart slow cooker, mix tomatoes, tomato liquid and remaining ingredients except cornstarch and water.

2 Cover and cook on low heat setting 8 to 10 hours.

3 In small bowl, mix cornstarch and water; gradually stir into stew until blended. Increase heat setting to high. Cover and cook about 20 minutes, stirring occasionally, until thickened.

1 Serving: Calories 150 (Calories from Fat 5); Total Fat 0.5g (Saturated Fat 0g); Cholesterol 0mg; Sodium 550mg; Total Carbohydrate 31g (Dietary Fiber 5g); Protein 4g

continental pork stew

Prep Time: 1 hr 10 min ▪ **Start to Finish:** 1 hr 10 min ▪ 6 Servings

1 tablespoon olive or vegetable oil

1 tablespoon butter or margarine

2 teaspoons finely chopped garlic

1 package (8 oz) sliced fresh mushrooms

1¹/₂ lb boneless pork loin roast, cut into 1-inch pieces

2¹/₂ cups chicken broth

1 cup white wine or chicken broth

1¹/₂ cups frozen pearl onions

3 medium carrots, cut lengthwise in half, then cut into ¹/₄-inch slices

1 small onion studded with 4 whole cloves*

1 teaspoon salt

¹/₈ teaspoon pepper

1 cup whipping cream

¹/₃ cup quick-mixing flour

Chopped fresh parsley, if desired

1 In 4¹/₂- to 5-quart Dutch oven, heat oil and butter over medium-high heat. Cook garlic and mushrooms in oil mixture 5 to 6 minutes, stirring frequently, until mushrooms are softened.

2 Stir in pork. Cook 6 to 7 minutes, stirring frequently, until pork is lightly browned.

3 Stir in broth, wine, pearl onions, carrots, onion with cloves, salt and pepper. Heat to boiling; reduce heat to medium-low. Cover and cook 25 to 30 minutes, stirring occasionally, until pork is tender and no longer pink in center.

4 Remove onion with cloves; discard. Beat in whipping cream and flour with whisk. Cook 5 to 6 minutes, stirring constantly, until hot and slightly thickened. Sprinkle with parsley.

*To make the studded onion for the stew, peel the onion, then gently push four whole cloves into it.

1 Serving: Calories 450 (Calories from Fat 270); Total Fat 30g (Saturated Fat 13g); Cholesterol 120mg; Sodium 910mg; Total Carbohydrate 15g (Dietary Fiber 2g); Protein 31g

zesty autumn pork stew

Prep Time: 25 min ▪ **Start to Finish:** 25 min ▪ 4 Servings

1 lb pork tenderloin, cut into 1-inch cubes

2 medium dark-orange sweet potatoes, peeled, cubed (2 cups)

1 medium green bell pepper, chopped (1 cup)

2 cloves garlic, finely chopped

1 cup coleslaw mix (shredded cabbage and carrots)

1 teaspoon Cajun seasoning

1 can (14 oz) chicken broth

1 Spray 4-quart Dutch oven with cooking spray; heat over medium-high heat. Cook pork in Dutch oven, stirring occasionally, until brown.

2 Stir in remaining ingredients. Heat to boiling; reduce heat. Cover; simmer about 15 minutes, stirring once, until sweet potatoes are tender.

1 Serving: Calories 240 (Calories from Fat 45); Total Fat 5g (Saturated Fat 2g); Cholesterol 70mg; Sodium 640mg; Total Carbohydrate 18g (Dietary Fiber 3g); Protein 30g

Canned vacuum-packed sweet potatoes, cubed, can be substituted for the fresh sweet potatoes. Add them after you reduce the heat in step 2, and remember to stir the mixture gently because canned sweet potatoes are very soft and tender.

curried coconut beef with winter vegetables

Prep Time: 25 min ■ **Start to Finish:** 1 hr 55 min ■ 6 Servings

1 tablespoon vegetable oil

2 lb beef stew meat

1 large onion, chopped (1 cup)

2 cloves garlic, finely chopped

1½ tablespoons curry powder

1 can (14 oz) coconut milk (not cream of coconut)

1 tablespoon packed brown sugar

2 tablespoons lemon juice

3 medium carrots, chopped (1½ cups)

2 medium parsnips, peeled, chopped (1 cup)

1½ cups chopped peeled sweet potatoes

1 teaspoon salt

¼ teaspoon pepper

Chopped fresh cilantro, if desired

1 Heat oven to 350°F. In 4-quart ovenproof Dutch oven, heat oil over medium-high heat. Cook beef in oil, stirring occasionally, until brown.

2 Stir in onion and garlic. Cook 2 to 3 minutes, stirring occasionally, until onion is crisp-tender. Stir in curry powder, coconut milk, brown sugar and lemon juice. Cover and place in oven; bake about 1 hour or until beef is tender.

3 Stir in remaining ingredients except cilantro. Cover and bake about 30 minutes or until vegetables are tender. Garnish with cilantro.

1 Serving: Calories 495 (Calories from Fat 260); Total Fat 29g (Saturated Fat 16g); Cholesterol 80mg; Sodium 510mg; Total Carbohydrate 35g (Dietary Fiber 7g); Protein 30g

This is perfect for a cozy winter supper. Add a crisp green salad, warm dinner rolls and hot coffee, cider or tea to round out the meal.

savory beef stew

Prep Time: 15 min ■ **Start to Finish:** 3 hr 45 min ■ 6 Servings

1¼ lb beef stew meat

1 medium onion, cut into 8 wedges

1 can (14.5 oz) stewed tomatoes, undrained

1¼ teaspoons seasoned salt

¼ teaspoon pepper

1 dried bay leaf

2 cups water

2 tablespoons all-purpose flour

12 small red potatoes (1¼ lb), cut in half

1 bag (8 oz) ready-to-eat baby-cut carrots (about 30)

1 Heat oven to 325°F. In ovenproof 4-quart Dutch oven, mix beef, onion, tomatoes, seasoned salt, pepper and bay leaf. In small bowl, mix water and flour; stir into beef mixture.

2 Cover and bake 2 hours, stirring once.

3 Stir in potatoes and carrots. Cover and bake 1 hour to 1 hour 30 minutes longer or until beef and vegetables are tender. Remove bay leaf.

1 Serving: Calories 350 (Calories from Fat 120); Total Fat 13g (Saturated Fat 5g); Cholesterol 70mg; Sodium 610mg; Total Carbohydrate 33g (Dietary Fiber 5g); Protein 26g

Add a bit of rich flavor, if you have the time, by browning the beef in a little oil before assembling the stew.

burgundy beef stew

Prep Time: 2 hr 5 min ▪ **Start to Finish:** 2 hr 5 min ▪ 8 Servings

6 slices bacon, cut into 1-inch pieces
2 lb beef stew meat, cut into 1-inch pieces
¹/₂ cup all-purpose flour
1¹/₂ cups dry red wine or beef broth
1¹/₂ teaspoons chopped fresh or ¹/₂ teaspoon dried thyme leaves
1¹/₄ teaspoons salt
1 teaspoon beef bouillon granules
¹/₄ teaspoon pepper
1 clove garlic, finely chopped
1 dried bay leaf
2 tablespoons butter or margarine
1 package (8 oz) sliced fresh mushrooms (3 cups)
4 medium onions, sliced
Chopped fresh parsley, if desired

1 In 4-quart Dutch oven, cook bacon over low heat, stirring occasionally, until crisp; remove bacon with slotted spoon. Refrigerate bacon.

2 Coat beef with flour. Cook beef in bacon drippings over medium-high heat, stirring frequently, until brown. Drain excess fat from Dutch oven.

3 Add wine and just enough water to cover beef in Dutch oven. Stir in thyme, salt, bouillon granules, pepper, garlic and bay leaf. Heat to boiling; reduce heat. Cover; simmer about 1 hour 30 minutes or until beef is tender.

4 In 12-inch skillet, melt butter over medium heat. Cook mushrooms and onions in butter, stirring frequently, until onions are tender. Stir mushroom mixture and bacon into stew. Cover; simmer 10 minutes. Remove bay leaf. Garnish stew with parsley.

1 Serving: Calories 340 (Calories from Fat 190); Total Fat 21g (Saturated Fat 8g); Cholesterol 85mg; Sodium 650mg; Total Carbohydrate 10g (Dietary Fiber 2g); Protein 27g

Serve the stew over hot cooked egg noodles for a complete meal in a bowl.

caramelized-onion pot roast

Prep Time: 25 min ∎ **Start to Finish:** 8 hr 25 min ∎ 6 Servings

2½ lb boneless beef chuck roast
½ teaspoon salt
¼ teaspoon pepper
1 tablespoon olive or vegetable oil
4 medium onions, sliced
1 cup beef broth
½ cup beer or apple juice
1 tablespoon packed brown sugar
1 tablespoon cider vinegar
2 tablespoons Dijon mustard
Horseradish, if desired

1 Spray 12-inch skillet with cooking spray; heat over medium-high heat. Cook beef in skillet 5 minutes, turning once, until brown. Add salt and pepper; remove from skillet.

2 Reduce heat to medium. Add oil to skillet. Cook onions in oil 12 to 14 minutes, stirring frequently, until brown. Stir in broth, beer, brown sugar, vinegar and mustard. Spoon half of the onion mixture into 4- to 5-quart slow cooker. Place beef roast on onions. Spoon remaining onion mixture onto beef.

3 Cover and cook on low heat setting 8 to 9 hours or until meat is tender.

4 Remove beef and onions from slow cooker and place on serving platter. Spoon some of the beef juices from slow cooker over beef. Serve with horseradish.

1 Serving: Calories 410 (Calories from Fat 215); Total Fat 24g (Saturated Fat 9g); Cholesterol 115mg; Sodium 530mg; Total Carbohydrate 10g (Dietary Fiber 2g); Protein 40g

In a hurry? Don't bother cooking the onions. Leave out the olive oil and mix the broth, beer, brown sugar, vinegar and mustard together. Place the onions in the slow cooker and top with beef and broth mixture.

mini meat loaves

Prep Time: 10 min ■ **Start to Finish:** 30 min ■ 6 Servings

$^{1}/_{2}$ **cup ketchup**

2 tablespoons packed brown sugar

1 lb lean (at least 80%) ground beef

$^{1}/_{2}$ **lb ground pork**

$^{1}/_{2}$ **cup Original Bisquick mix**

$^{1}/_{2}$ **teaspoon pepper**

1 small onion, finely chopped ($^{1}/_{4}$ cup)

1 egg

1 Heat oven to 450°F. In small bowl, stir ketchup and brown sugar until mixed; reserve $^{1}/_{4}$ cup for topping. In large bowl, stir remaining ingredients and remaining ketchup mixture until well mixed.

2 Spray 13×9-inch pan with cooking spray. Place meat mixture in pan; pat into 12×4-inch rectangle. Cut lengthwise down center and then crosswise into sixths to form 12 loaves. Separate loaves, using spatula, so no edges are touching. Brush loaves with reserved $^{1}/_{4}$ cup ketchup mixture.

3 Bake 18 to 20 minutes or until meat thermometer inserted in center of loaves reads 160°F.

1 Serving (2 loaves each): Calories 300 (Calories from Fat 140); Total Fat 16g (Saturated Fat 6g); Cholesterol 105mg; Sodium 430mg; Total Carbohydrate 16g (Dietary Fiber 0g); Protein 22g

So cute! These little loaves bake much faster than the traditional loaf shape. Make that 30 minutes versus an hour or so!

grandma's macaroni and cheese

Prep Time: 25 min ■ **Start to Finish:** 50 min ■ 4 Servings

2 cups uncooked elbow macaroni (7 oz)
$1/4$ cup butter
$1/4$ cup all-purpose flour
$1/2$ teaspoon salt
$1/4$ teaspoon pepper
$1/4$ teaspoon ground mustard
$1/4$ teaspoon Worcestershire sauce
2 cups milk
2 cups shredded sharp Cheddar cheese (8 oz)

1 Heat oven to 350°F. Cook and drain macaroni as directed on package.

2 Meanwhile, in 3-quart saucepan, melt butter over low heat. Stir in flour, salt, pepper, mustard and Worcestershire sauce. Cook over low heat, stirring constantly, until mixture is smooth and bubbly; remove from heat. Stir in milk. Heat to boiling, stirring constantly. Boil and stir 1 minute; remove from heat. Stir in cheese until melted.

3 Gently stir macaroni into cheese sauce. Pour into ungreased 2-quart casserole.

4 Bake uncovered 20 to 25 minutes or until bubbly.

1 Serving: Calories 610 (Calories from Fat 300); Total Fat 34g (Saturated Fat 19g); Cholesterol 100mg; Sodium 790mg; Total Carbohydrate 51g (Dietary Fiber 3g); Protein 26g

Add surprise to your mac n' cheese—mix up your cheeses! Try Jarlsberg, smoked Gouda or white Cheddar for all or half of the sharp Cheddar.

chili beef 'n pasta

Prep Time: 20 min ∎ **Start to Finish:** 20 min ∎ 4 Servings

2¹/₂ **cups uncooked rotini pasta (8 oz)**
1 **lb lean (at least 80%) ground beef**
1 **medium onion, chopped (¹/₂ cup)**
1 **can (11.25 oz) condensed fiesta chili beef with beans soup**
1 **jar (8 oz) chunky-style salsa (1 cup)**
¹/₂ **cup water**
1 **cup shredded Cheddar cheese (4 oz)**

1 Cook and drain pasta as directed on package.

2 Meanwhile, in 12-inch skillet, cook beef and onion over medium-high heat, stirring occasionally, until beef is thoroughly-cooked; drain. Reduce heat to medium. Stir soup, salsa and water into beef. Cook until thoroughly heated.

3 Serve beef mixture over pasta. Sprinkle with cheese.

1 Serving: Calories 660 (Calories from Fat 240); Total Fat 26g (Saturated Fat 12g); Cholesterol 110mg; Sodium 1260mg; Total Carbohydrate 65g (Dietary Fiber 6g); Protein 40g

manicotti

Prep Time: 40 min ▪ **Start to Finish:** 1 hr 35 min ▪ 7 Servings

14 uncooked manicotti shells
1 lb lean (at least 80%) ground beef
1 large onion, chopped (1 cup)
2 cloves garlic, finely chopped
1 jar (26 to 30 oz) tomato pasta sauce (any variety)
2 boxes (10 oz each) frozen chopped spinach, thawed
2 cups small curd cottage cheese
2 cans (4 oz each) mushroom pieces and stems, drained
¹/₃ cup grated Parmesan cheese
¹/₄ teaspoon ground nutmeg
¹/₄ teaspoon pepper
2 cups shredded mozzarella cheese (8 oz)
2 tablespoons grated Parmesan cheese

1 Cook and drain manicotti as directed on package using minimum cooking time (cooking for the minimum time helps prevent the shells from tearing while filling).

2 Meanwhile, in 10-inch skillet, cook beef, onion and garlic over medium heat 8 to 10 minutes, stirring occasionally, until beef is thorougly cooked; drain. Stir in pasta sauce.

3 Heat oven to 350°F. Spray 13×9-inch (3-quart) glass baking dish with cooking spray.

4 Squeeze thawed spinach to drain; spread on paper towels and pat dry. In medium bowl, mix spinach, cottage cheese, mushrooms, ¹/₃ cup Parmesan cheese, the nutmeg and pepper.

5 In baking dish, spread 1 cup of the beef mixture. Fill manicotti shells with spinach mixture. Place shells on beef mixture in dish. Pour remaining beef mixture evenly over shells, covering shells completely. Sprinkle with mozzarella cheese and 2 tablespoons Parmesan cheese.

6 Cover and bake 30 minutes. Uncover and bake 20 to 25 minutes longer or until hot and bubbly.

1 Serving: Calories 570 (Calories from Fat 190); Total Fat 21g (Saturated Fat 10g); Cholesterol 70mg; Sodium 1360mg; Total Carbohydrate 55g (Dietary Fiber 6g); Protein 39g

ravioli and vegetables with pesto cream

Prep Time: 20 min ■ **Start to Finish:** 20 min ■ 4 Servings

2 teaspoons olive or vegetable oil

8 oz green beans, cut into 1¹/₂-inch pieces

¹/₂ medium yellow bell pepper, cut into ¹/₂-inch pieces (¹/₂ cup)

3 plum (Roma) tomatoes, cut into ¹/₂-inch pieces (1 cup)

¹/₂ teaspoon salt

16 oz frozen cheese-filled ravioli (from 25 to 27.5 oz package)

¹/₂ cup sour cream

3 tablespoons basil pesto

2 teaspoons grated lemon peel

1 In 12-inch nonstick skillet, heat oil over medium-high heat. Cook green beans and bell pepper in oil about 5 minutes, stirring frequently, until crisp-tender. Stir in tomatoes and salt. Cook 3 minutes.

2 Meanwhile, cook ravioli as directed on package. In small bowl, mix sour cream, basil pesto and lemon peel.

3 Drain ravioli; return to saucepan. Toss ravioli, vegetable mixture and sour cream mixture.

1 Serving: Calories 380 (Calories from Fat 210); Total Fat 24g (Saturated Fat 9g); Cholesterol 135mg; Sodium 1350mg; Total Carbohydrate 26g (Dietary Fiber 3g); Protein 16g

asian noodle bowl

Prep Time: 30 min ▪ **Start to Finish:** 30 min ▪ 4 Servings

$^1/_4$ **cup barbecue sauce**

2 tablespoons hoisin sauce

1 tablespoon peanut butter

Dash of ground red pepper (cayenne), if desired

1 tablespoon vegetable oil

1 small onion, cut into thin wedges

$^1/_4$ **cup chopped red bell pepper**

2 cups broccoli florets

$^3/_4$ **cup water**

$^1/_2$ **teaspoon salt, if desired**

1 package (10 oz) Chinese curly noodles

1 can (14 oz) baby corn cobs, drained

$^1/_4$ **cup chopped peanuts**

1 In medium bowl, mix barbecue sauce, hoisin sauce, peanut butter and ground red pepper; set aside.

2 In 12-inch skillet, heat oil over medium heat 1 to 2 minutes. Cook onion and bell pepper in oil 2 minutes, stirring frequently. Stir in broccoli and $^3/_4$ cup water. Cover and cook 4 to 6 minutes, stirring occasionally, until broccoli is crisp-tender.

3 Meanwhile, fill 4-quart Dutch oven about half full with water; add salt. Cover and heat to boiling over high heat. Add noodles; heat to boiling. Boil uncovered 4 to 5 minutes, stirring frequently, until noodles are tender.

4 While noodles are cooking, stir corn and sauce mixture into vegetable mixture. Cook uncovered 3 to 4 minutes, stirring occasionally, until mixture is hot and bubbly.

5 Drain noodles. Divide noodles among 4 individual serving bowls. Spoon vegetable mixture over noodles. Sprinkle with peanuts.

1 Serving: Calories 520 (Calories from Fat 130); Total Fat 14g (Saturated Fat 2.5g); Cholesterol 60mg; Sodium 980mg; Total Carbohydrate 80g (Dietary Fiber 7g); Protein 17g

pork lo mein

Prep Time: 25 min ▪ **Start to Finish:** 25 min ▪ 4 servings

$1/2$ lb boneless pork loin

$2^{1}/_{2}$ cups sugar snap pea pods

$1^{1}/_{2}$ cups ready-to-eat baby-cut carrots, cut lengthwise into $1/4$-inch sticks

$1/2$ package (9-oz size) refrigerated linguine, cut into 2-inch pieces

$1/3$ cup chicken broth

1 tablespoon soy sauce

2 teaspoons cornstarch

1 teaspoon sugar

2 teaspoons finely chopped gingerroot

2 to 4 cloves garlic, finely chopped

2 teaspoons canola oil

$1/2$ cup thinly sliced red onion

Toasted sesame seed, if desired*

1 Trim fat from pork. Cut pork with grain into 2×1-inch strips; cut strips across grain into $1/8$-inch slices (pork is easier to cut if partially frozen, about 1 hour 30 minutes). Remove strings from pea pods.

2 In 3-quart saucepan, heat 2 quarts water to boiling. Add pea pods, carrots and linguine; heat to boiling. Boil 2 to 3 minutes or just until linguine is tender; drain.

3 In small bowl, mix broth, soy sauce, cornstarch, sugar, gingerroot and garlic.

4 In 12-inch nonstick skillet or wok, heat oil over medium-high heat. Add pork and onion; stir-fry about 2 minutes or until pork is no longer pink. Stir broth mixture; stir into pork mixture. Stir in pea pods, carrots and linguine. Cook 2 minutes, stirring occasionally. Sprinkle with sesame seed.

*To toast sesame seed, sprinkle in an ungreased heavy skillet and cook over medium-low heat 5 to 7 minutes, stirring frequently until browning begins, then stirring constantly until golden brown.

1 Serving: Calories 200 (Calories from Fat 45): Total Fat 5g (Saturated Fat 1g): Cholesterol 35mg; Sodium 370mg; Total Carbohydrate 21g (Dietary Fiber 4g): Protein 17g

four-cheese mashed potato casserole

Prep Time: 25 min ∎ **Start to Finish:** 1 hr 35 min ∎ 24 Servings

5 lb white potatoes, peeled, cut into 1-inch pieces (about 14 cups)

3 oz (from 8-oz package) reduced-fat cream cheese (Neufchâtel), softened

¼ cup crumbled blue cheese

1 cup shredded reduced-fat Cheddar cheese (4 oz)

¼ cup shredded Parmesan cheese

1 container (8 oz) reduced-fat sour cream

1 teaspoon garlic salt

¼ teaspoon paprika

1 teaspoon chopped fresh chives, if desired

1 In 6-quart saucepan or Dutch oven, place potatoes. Add enough water to cover potatoes. Heat to boiling over high heat; reduce heat to medium. Cook uncovered 15 to 18 minutes or until tender; drain. Mash potatoes in saucepan with potato masher or electric mixer on low speed.

2 Meanwhile, in large bowl, beat cream cheese, blue cheese, Cheddar cheese and Parmesan cheese with electric mixer on low speed until smooth. Beat in sour cream and garlic salt.

3 Heat oven to 350°F. Stir cheese mixture into mashed potatoes until well blended. If potatoes are too stiff, stir in milk, 1 tablespoon at a time, until desired consistency. Spoon into ungreased 13×9-inch (3-quart) glass baking dish.

4 Bake uncovered 35 to 40 minutes or until hot and top is lightly browned. Sprinkle with paprika and chives.

1 Serving (½ cup each): Calories 110 (Calories from Fat 25): Total Fat 3g (Saturated Fat 2g); Cholesterol 10mg; Sodium 140mg: Total Carbohydrate 18g (Dietary Fiber 2g); Protein 4g

Cheese and potatoes—a marriage made in heaven!

garden ratatouille

Prep Time: 25 min ▪ **Start to Finish:** 25 min ▪ 8 Servings

3 cups ¹/₂-inch cubes eggplant (1 lb)

1 small zucchini, cut into ¹/₄-inch slices (1 cup)

1 small onion, sliced

¹/₂ medium green bell pepper, cut into strips

2 cloves garlic, finely chopped

2 tablespoons chopped fresh parsley

1 tablespoon chopped fresh or ¹/₂ teaspoon dried basil leaves

2 tablespoons water

¹/₂ teaspoon salt

¹/₄ teaspoon pepper

2 medium very ripe tomatoes, cut into eighths

1 In 10-inch skillet, cook all ingredients except tomatoes over medium heat about 10 minutes, stirring occasionally, until vegetables are tender; remove from heat.

2 Stir in tomatoes. (For added flavor, drizzle with about 2 tablespoons olive oil, if desired.) Cover and let stand 2 to 3 minutes until tomatoes are warm.

1 Serving: Calories 25 (Calories from Fat 0): Total Fat 0g (Saturated Fat 0g); Cholesterol 0mg; Sodium 150mg; Total Carbohydrate 5g (Dietary Fiber 2g); Protein 0g

This is a great summer recipe, though you can feel free to make it any time of year.

9
decadent desserts

orange sorbet and raspberry parfaits

Prep Time: 15 min ∎ **Start to Finish:** 15 min ∎ 4 Servings

1 pint (2 cups) fresh raspberries

2 tablespoons sugar

2 tablespoons orange or raspberry liqueur

4 slices (about $^3/_4$ inch thick) frozen pound cake (from 10.75-oz package), thawed

1 pint (2 cups) orange sorbet

1 Reserve about $^1/_4$ cup of the raspberries for garnish. In medium bowl, mix remaining raspberries, the sugar and liqueur.

2 Cut pound cake into $^3/_4$-inch cubes. In each of 4 parfait glasses, layer half of the cake, half of the sorbet and half of the raspberry mixture. Repeat layers. Sprinkle with reserved raspberries. Serve immediately.

1 Serving: Calories 520 (Calories from Fat 170); Total Fat 19g (Saturated Fat 8g); Cholesterol 80mg; Sodium 80mg; Total Carbohydrate 83g (Dietary Fiber 5g); Protein 5g

If you don't have parfait glasses, layer this dessert in champagne or wine goblets or fancy dessert dishes. Add a touch of color with a sprig of fresh mint.

fresh peach cobbler

Prep Time: 30 min ▪ **Start to Finish:** 1 hr ▪ 6 Servings

1/2 cup sugar

1 tablespoon cornstarch

1/4 teaspoon ground cinnamon

4 cups sliced fresh peaches (6 medium)

1 teaspoon lemon juice

1 cup all-purpose flour

1 tablespoon sugar

1 1/2 teaspoons baking powder

1/2 teaspoon salt

3 tablespoons firm butter or margarine

1/2 cup milk

2 tablespoons sugar, if desired

Sweetened whipped cream, if desired

1 Heat oven to 400°F.

2 In 2-quart saucepan, mix 1/2 cup sugar, the cornstarch and cinnamon. Stir in peaches and lemon juice. Cook over medium-high heat 4 to 5 minutes, stirring constantly, until mixture thickens and boils. Boil and stir 1 minute. Pour into ungreased 2-quart casserole; keep peach mixture hot in oven.

3 In medium bowl, mix flour, 1 tablespoon sugar, the baking powder and salt. Cut in butter, using pastry blender (or pulling 2 table knives through ingredients in opposite directions), until mixture looks like fine crumbs. Stir in milk. Drop dough by 6 spoonfuls onto hot peach mixture. Sprinkle 2 tablespoons sugar over dough.

4 Bake 25 to 30 minutes or until topping is golden brown. Serve warm with sweetened whipped cream.

1 Serving: Calories 300 (Calories from Fat 120); Total Fat 13g (Saturated Fat 7g); Cholesterol 40mg; Sodium 240mg; Total Carbohydrate 44g (Dietary Fiber 4g); Protein 3g

Cobblers are a homey way to use fruit in season. Short on time? Try the blueberry variation—there's no peeling or pitting! Substitute 4 cups blueberries for the peaches. Omit the cinnamon.

roasted almond–cranberry-pear crisp

Prep Time: 25 min ■ **Start to Finish:** 1 hr 30 min ■ 8 Servings

5 cups sliced peeled pears (5 to 6 pears)

2 cups fresh or frozen cranberries

1 cup granulated sugar

3 tablespoons all-purpose flour

6 roasted almond crunchy granola bars (3 pouches from 8.9-oz box), finely crushed

¹⁄₂ cup all-purpose flour

¹⁄₄ cup packed brown sugar

¹⁄₄ cup butter or margarine, melted

Whipped cream or vanilla ice cream, if desired

1 Heat oven to 350°F. Spray 8-inch square (2-quart) glass baking dish with cooking spray. In large bowl, mix pears, cranberries, granulated sugar and 3 tablespoons flour. Spoon evenly into baking dish.

2 In medium bowl, mix crushed granola bars, ½ cup flour, the brown sugar and butter until crumbly. Sprinkle over pear mixture.

3 Bake 55 to 65 minutes or until top is golden brown and fruit is tender (mixture will be bubbly). Cool slightly. Serve warm or cool with whipped cream or ice cream.

1 Serving: Calories 370 (Calories from Fat 80); Total Fat 9g (Saturated Fat 3g); Cholesterol 15mg; Sodium 100mg; Total Carbohydrate 69g (Dietary Fiber 5g); Protein 3g

You can crush the granola bars right in their pouches or crush them in a food processor.

sour cream–pear fold-over pie

Prep Time: 30 min ▪ **Start to Finish:** 1 hr 35 min ▪ 8 Servings

Filling
$^2/_3$ cup sugar

$^1/_2$ cup sour cream

$^1/_2$ cup golden or dark raisins

$^1/_4$ cup all-purpose flour

1 teaspoon ground cinnamon

4 cups $^1/_2$-inch slices peeled pears (about
   3 medium)

Pastry
1 cup all-purpose flour

$^1/_2$ teaspoon salt

$^1/_3$ cup plus 1 tablespoon shortening

2 to 3 tablespoons cold water

Topping
$^1/_4$ cup coarsely chopped walnuts

1 to 2 tablespoons milk, if desired

1 tablespoon sugar, if desired

1 Heat oven to 425°F. In large bowl, stir all filling ingredients except pears until mixed. Fold in pears; set aside.

2 In medium bowl, mix 1 cup flour and the salt. Cut in shortening, using pastry blender (or pulling 2 knives through mixture in opposite directions), until mixture looks like fine crumbs. Sprinkle with cold water, 1 tablespoon at a time, tossing with fork until all flour is moistened and pastry almost cleans side of bowl (1 to 2 teaspoons more water can be added if necessary).

3 Gather pastry into a ball. Shape into flattened round on lightly floured surface. Roll pastry into 13-inch round. Place on ungreased large cookie sheet.

4 Mound filling on center of pastry to within 3 inches of edge. Sprinkle walnuts over filling. Fold edge of pastry over filling, overlapping to make about 12 pleats and leaving 6-inch circle of filling showing in center. Brush milk over pastry; sprinkle with 1 tablespoon sugar.

5 Bake 30 to 35 minutes, covering crust with foil for the last 10 to 15 minutes to prevent burning if necessary, until crust is golden brown and filling is bubbly in center. Cool 30 minutes. Cut into wedges. Serve warm.

1 Serving: Calories 370 (Calories from Fat 140); Total Fat 16g (Saturated Fat 4.5g); Cholesterol 10mg; Sodium 150mg; Total Carbohydrate 52g (Dietary Fiber 4g); Protein 4g

fabulous three-berry tart

Prep Time: 30 min ■ **Start to Finish:** 2 hr 30 min ■ 10 Servings

Crust
1 bag (8 oz) animal crackers

¹/₃ cup butter or margarine, melted

1 teaspoon ground cinnamon

2 tablespoons sugar

Filling
1 package (8 oz) cream cheese, softened

¹/₂ cup sugar

2 tablespoons lemon juice

1 cup whipping cream

¹/₂ pint (1 cup) fresh blackberries

¹/₂ pint (1 cup) fresh raspberries

¹/₂ pint (1 cup) fresh blueberries

¹/₄ cup strawberry jam

1 tablespoon orange juice

1 Heat oven to 350°F. Place animal crackers in food processor; cover and process about 1 minute or until finely ground. In medium bowl, mix cracker crumbs, butter, cinnamon and 2 tablespoons sugar. Press mixture evenly in bottom and up side of ungreased 9-inch tart pan with removable bottom. Bake 8 to 12 minutes or until golden brown. Cool completely, about 20 minutes.

2 Meanwhile, in large bowl, beat cream cheese, ½ cup sugar and the lemon juice with electric mixer on low speed until blended. Add whipping cream; beat on high speed 3 to 5 minutes or until light and fluffy. Spread mixture in tart shell. Refrigerate at least 2 hours.

3 Arrange berries on chilled filling. In small microwavable bowl, microwave jam uncovered on High about 20 seconds or until warm. Stir in orange juice; mix well with fork. Brush strawberry glaze over berries.

1 Serving: Calories 410 (Calories from Fat 220); Total Fat 25g (Saturated Fat 14g); Cholesterol 70mg; Sodium 220mg; Total Carbohydrate 41g (Dietary Fiber 3g); Protein 4g

dutch apple wedges

Prep Time: 25 min ■ **Start to Finish:** 1 hr 35 min ■ 12 Servings

Crust
1 cup all-purpose flour

$^1/_3$ cup sugar

$^1/_2$ cup butter or margarine

Crumb Topping
$^2/_3$ cup all-purpose flour

$^1/_2$ cup packed brown sugar

$^1/_4$ cup butter or margarine

Apple Topping
$^1/_3$ cup sugar

2 tablespoons all-purpose flour

$^3/_4$ teaspoon ground cinnamon

$1^1/_2$ cups thinly sliced peeled tart cooking apples

1 Heat oven to 350°F. In medium bowl, mix 1 cup flour and $^1/_3$ cup sugar. Cut in $^1/_2$ cup butter, using pastry blender (or pulling 2 knives through mixture in opposite directions), until mixture looks like fine crumbs. Press mixture evenly in bottom of ungreased 9-inch round pan. Bake 25 minutes.

2 Meanwhile, in small bowl, mix all topping ingredients until crumbly; set aside.

3 In medium bowl, mix $^1/_3$ cup sugar, 2 tablespoons flour and the cinnamon. Stir in apples until coated. Spoon apple mixture over baked crust. Sprinkle with topping.

4 Bake about 30 minutes or until topping is light brown and apples are tender. Cool 30 minutes before serving. Serve warm or cool. Cut into 12 wedges.

1 Serving: Calories 260 (Calories from Fat 110); Total Fat 12g (Saturated Fat 6g); Cholesterol 30mg; Sodium 80mg; Total Carbohydrate 36g (Dietary Fiber 0g); Protein 2g

Tart cooking apples perfect for this dessert include Granny Smith, Greening and Haralson.

crème brûlée

Prep Time: 20 min ▪ **Start to Finish:** 7 hr ▪ 4 Servings

6 egg yolks
2 cups whipping cream
$^1/_3$ cup granulated sugar
1 teaspoon vanilla
Boiling water
8 teaspoons brown sugar

1 Heat oven to 350°F. In small bowl, slightly beat egg yolks with whisk. In large bowl, stir whipping cream, $^1/_3$ cup granulated sugar and the vanilla until well mixed. Add egg yolks to cream mixture; beat with whisk until evenly colored and well blended.

2 In 13×9-inch pan, place four 6-oz ceramic ramekins.* Divide cream mixture evenly among ramekins.

3 Carefully place pan with ramekins in oven. Pour enough boiling water into pan, being careful not to splash water into ramekins, until water covers two-thirds of the height of the ramekins.

4 Bake 30 to 40 minutes or until top is light golden brown and sides are set (centers will be jiggly).

5 Carefully transfer ramekins to wire rack, using tongs or grasping tops of ramekins with pot holder. Cool 2 hours or until room temperature. Cover tightly with plastic wrap and refrigerate until chilled, at least 4 hours but no longer than 2 days.

6 To make caramelized crust, turn on broiler. Uncover ramekins; gently blot any condensation on custards with paper towel. Sprinkle 2 teaspoons sugar over each custard. Place ramekins in 15×10×1-inch pan or on cookie sheet with sides. Broil with tops 4 to 6 inches from heat 5 to 6 minutes or until sugar is melted and forms a glaze. Serve immediately, or refrigerate up to 8 hours before serving.

*Do not use glass custard cups or glass pie plates; they cannot withstand the heat from the broiler and may break.

1 Serving: Calories 540 (Calories from Fat 400); Total Fat 45g (Saturated Fat 25g); Cholesterol 450mg; Sodium 50mg; Total Carbohydrate 29g (Dietary Fiber 0g); Protein 7g

dark chocolate raspberry fondue

Prep Time: 20 min ▪ **Start to Finish:** 20 min ▪ 16 Servings

²/₃ **cup whipping cream**
¹/₃ **cup seedless raspberry preserves**
1 tablespoon honey
1 bag (12 oz) semisweet chocolate chunks
**Assorted dippers (fresh fruit pieces, pretzels, shortbread cookies, pound cake cubes or angel food cake
cubes), if desired**

1 In fondue pot or 2-quart saucepan, mix whipping cream, raspberry preserves and honey. Heat over
warm/simmer setting or medium-low heat, stirring occasionally, just until bubbles rise to surface
(do not boil).

2 Add chocolate; stir with wire whisk until melted. Keep warm over warm/simmer setting. (If using
saucepan, pour into fondue pot and keep warm over warm/simmer setting.) Serve with dippers.

1 Serving (2 tablespoons each): Calories 155 (Calories from Fat 80); Total Fat 9g (Saturated Fat 6g); Cholesterol 10mg; Sodium 10mg; Total Carbohydrate
19g (Dietary Fiber 1g); Protein 1g

No fondue pot? Just serve the fondue in a shallow bowl instead of a fondue pot.

chocolate mousse

Prep Time: 30 min ▪ **Start to Finish:** 2 hr 40 min ▪ 8 Servings

Mousse
4 egg yolks

¼ cup sugar

2½ cups whipping cream

8 oz semisweet baking chocolate, chopped

Chocolate Piping
½ cup semisweet chocolate chips

½ teaspoon shortening

1 In small bowl, beat egg yolks with electric mixer on high speed about 3 minutes or until thickened and lemon colored. Gradually beat in sugar.

2 In 2-quart saucepan, heat 1 cup of the whipping cream over medium heat just until hot. Gradually stir half of the hot cream into egg yolk mixture, then stir egg mixture back into hot cream in saucepan. Cook over low heat about 5 minutes, stirring constantly, until mixture thickens (do not boil).

3 Stir in baking chocolate until melted. Cover; refrigerate about 2 hours, stirring occasionally, just until chilled.

4 In chilled medium bowl, beat remaining 1½ cups whipping cream on high speed until stiff peaks form. Fold chocolate mixture into whipped cream.

5 In 1-cup microwavable measuring cup, microwave chocolate chips and shortening uncovered on medium 30 seconds. Stir; microwave in 10-second increments, stirring after each, until melted and smooth. Place in small resealable food-storage plastic bag; seal bag. Cut off tiny corner of bag. Squeeze bag to pipe designs or swirls inside parfait glasses. Refrigerate 10 minutes to set chocolate.

6 Spoon mousse into decorated glasses. Refrigerate until serving.

1 Serving: Calories 490 (Calories from Fat 330); Total Fat 37g (Saturated Fat 22g); Cholesterol 185mg; Sodium 35mg; Total Carbohydrate 33g (Dietary Fiber 2g); Protein 5g

The cream will whip up faster if you chill the bowl and beaters in the freezer for about 15 minutes before whipping.

fudge crinkles

Prep Time: 1 hr ■ **Start to Finish:** 1 hr ■ 30 Cookies

1 package devil's food cake mix with pudding in the mix
¹/₂ cup vegetable oil
2 eggs
1 teaspoon vanilla
¹/₃ cup powdered sugar

1 Heat oven to 350°F. In large bowl, mix cake mix, oil, eggs and vanilla with spoon until dough forms.

2 Shape dough into 1-inch balls. Roll balls in powdered sugar. On ungreased cookie sheet, place balls about 2 inches apart.

3 Bake 10 to 12 minutes or until set. Cool 1 minute; remove from cookie sheet to cooling rack. Cool completely, about 30 minutes. Store tightly covered.

1 Cookie: Calories 110 (Calories from Fat 45); Total Fat 5g (Saturated Fat 1g); Cholesterol 15mg; Sodium 140mg; Total Carbohydrate 15g (Dietary Fiber 0g); Protein 1g

For extra fun, stir 1 cup mini candy-coated chocolate baking bits into the dough.

rocky road bars

Prep Time: 15 min ■ **Start to Finish:** 1 hr 50 min ■ 24 Bars

1 package chocolate fudge or devil's food cake mix with pudding in the mix

¹/₂ cup butter or margarine, melted

¹/₃ cup water

¹/₄ cup packed brown sugar

2 eggs

1 cup chopped nuts

3 cups miniature marshmallows

¹/₂ cup pastel colored candy-coated chocolate candies, if desired

¹/₃ cup chocolate frosting (from 1-lb container)

1 Heat oven to 350°F. Spray bottom and sides of 13×9-inch pan with baking spray with flour.

2 In large bowl, mix half of the cake mix, the butter, water, brown sugar and eggs with spoon until smooth. Stir in remaining cake mix and the nuts. Spread in pan.

3 Bake 20 minutes; sprinkle with marshmallows. Bake 10 to 15 minutes longer or until marshmallows are puffed and golden. Sprinkle with candies.

4 In small microwavable bowl, microwave frosting uncovered on High 15 seconds; drizzle over bars. Cool completely, about 1 hour. For easier cutting, use plastic knife dipped in hot water. Cut into 6 rows by 4 rows. Store covered.

1 Bar: Calories 210 (Calories from Fat 90); Total Fat 10g (Saturated Fat 3.5g); Cholesterol 30mg; Sodium 220mg; Total Carbohydrate 28g (Dietary Fiber 0g); Protein 2g

You can use any kind of nuts, but peanuts are classic in rocky road recipes.

tiny lemon gem tarts

Prep Time: 1 hr 30 min ▪ **Start to Finish:** 2 hr 15 min ▪ 24 Tarts

$^1/_2$ **cup butter or margarine, softened**

3 tablespoons granulated sugar

1 cup all-purpose flour

$^1/_2$ **cup granulated sugar**

1 tablespoon all-purpose flour

3 tablespoons fresh lemon juice

2 teaspoons grated lemon peel

$^1/_4$ **teaspoon baking powder**

$^1/_8$ **teaspoon salt**

2 eggs

2 tablespoons powdered sugar

Additional powdered sugar, if desired

1 Heat oven to 350°F. Spray 24 mini muffin cups with cooking spray. In medium bowl, beat butter and 3 tablespoons granulated sugar with electric mixer on medium speed until well mixed. Beat in 1 cup flour until dough forms.

2 Shape dough into $^3/_4$-inch balls. Press 1 ball in bottom and up side of each muffin cup for crust. Bake 14 to 16 minutes or until edges begin to turn golden brown.

3 Meanwhile, in same bowl, beat remaining ingredients except powdered sugar on medium speed until well mixed.

4 Spoon 1 heaping tablespoon mixture evenly into each baked crust. Bake 10 to 12 minutes or until filling is light golden. Cool in pan 15 minutes; remove from pan to cooling racks. Cool completely, about 30 minutes.

5 Sift 2 tablespoons powdered sugar over tops of tarts. Store covered in refrigerator. Sift additional powdered sugar over tarts just before serving.

Do Ahead: To freeze, arrange in a single layer on cookie sheets and freeze until firm. Then pop them in an airtight container and store in the freezer. To thaw, let stand at room temperature for 30 minutes.

1 Tart: Calories 90 (Calories from Fat 40); Total Fat 4.5g (Saturated Fat 2.5g); Cholesterol 30mg; Sodium 50mg; Total Carbohydrate 11g (Dietary Fiber 0g); Protein 1g

caramel pecan cheesecake bites

Prep Time: 15 min ▪ **Start to Finish:** 3 hr 30 min ▪ 70 Bites

Graham Cracker Crust
1¹/₂ cups graham cracker crumbs

¹/₄ cup sugar

¹/₄ cup butter or margarine, melted

Cheesecake Bites
3 packages (8 oz each) cream cheese, softened

²/₃ cup granulated sugar

1 teaspoon vanilla

¹/₄ cup whipping cream

3 eggs

¹/₂ cup pecan halves, coarsely chopped

1 tablespoon butter or margarine, softened

1 tablespoon packed brown sugar

¹/₃ cup caramel topping

1 Heat oven to 325°F. Line 15×10×1-inch pan with foil. In medium bowl, mix all crust ingredients. Press in bottom of pan, using fork. Bake 8 to 10 minutes; cool.

2 In large bowl, beat cream cheese with electric mixer on medium speed until smooth. Gradually beat in granulated sugar and the vanilla until smooth. Beat in whipping cream. Beat in eggs, one at a time. Pour over crust. In small bowl, stir pecans, butter, brown sugar and caramel topping until mixed; drop evenly over cheesecake.

3 Bake 30 to 35 minutes or until set and light golden brown around edges. Let stand 30 minutes to cool. Cover and refrigerate at least 2 hours but no longer than 48 hours. Cut cheesecake with 1¹/₄-inch round cookie cutter; place on serving plate. Drizzle with additional caramel topping if desired.

1 Bite: Calories 95 (Calories from Fat 45); Total Fat 5g (Saturated Fat 3g); Cholesterol 20mg; Sodium 105mg; Total Carbohydrate 11g (Dietary Fiber 0g); Protein 2g

caramel-carrot cake

Prep Time: 10 min ▪ **Start to Finish:** 3 hr ▪ 15 Servings

1 package carrot cake mix with pudding in the mix
1 cup water
$^1/_3$ cup butter or margarine, melted
3 eggs
1 jar (16 to 17.5 oz) caramel or butterscotch topping
1 container (1 lb) vanilla creamy ready-to-spread frosting

1 Heat oven to 350°F. Grease bottom only of 13×9-inch pan with shortening or spray bottom with cooking spray.

2 In large bowl, beat cake mix, water, butter and eggs with electric mixer on low speed 30 seconds. Beat on medium speed 2 minutes. Pour into pan.

3 Bake 27 to 33 minutes or until toothpick inserted in center comes out clean. Cool 15 minutes. Poke top of warm cake every $^1/_2$ inch with handle of wooden spoon, wiping handle occasionally to reduce sticking. Reserve $^1/_2$ cup caramel topping. Drizzle remaining caramel topping evenly over top of cake; let stand about 15 minutes or until caramel topping has been absorbed into cake. Run knife around side of pan to loosen cake. Cover and refrigerate about 2 hours or until chilled.

4 Set aside 2 tablespoons of the reserved $^1/_2$ cup caramel topping. Stir remaining topping into frosting; spread over top of cake. Drizzle with reserved 2 tablespoons caramel topping. Store covered in refrigerator.

1 Serving: Calories 450 (Calories from Fat 120); Total Fat 13g (Saturated Fat 7g); Cholesterol 55mg; Sodium 430mg; Total Carbohydrate 79g (Dietary Fiber 0g); Protein 3g

This gooey, rich cake needs to be joined by only a glass of milk or a cup of steaming coffee.

lemon–poppy seed bundt cake

Prep Time: 15 min ∎ **Start to Finish:** 3 hr 10 min ∎ 16 Servings

Cake
1 package lemon cake mix with pudding in the mix

1¼ cups water

⅓ cup vegetable oil

3 eggs

2 tablespoons poppy seed

Lemon Glaze
1 cup powdered sugar

1 to 2 tablespoons lemon juice

¼ teaspoon grated lemon peel

Grated lemon peel, if desired

1 Heat oven to 350°F. Grease 12-cup fluted tube cake pan with shortening; lightly flour.

2 In large bowl, beat cake mix, water, oil and eggs with electric mixer on low speed 30 seconds. Beat on medium speed 2 minutes, scraping bowl occasionally. Stir poppy seed into batter. Pour into pan.

3 Bake 38 to 43 minutes or until toothpick inserted in center comes out clean. Cool in pan 10 minutes. Turn pan upside down onto wire rack or heatproof serving plate; remove pan. Cool completely, about 2 hours.

4 In a small bowl, stir powdered sugar, 1 tablespoon lemon juice and the lemon peel until blended. Stir in additional lemon juice, 1 teaspoon at a time, until smooth and consistency of thick syrup. Spread glaze over top of cake, allowing some to drizzle down side. Garnish with lemon peel. Store loosely covered at room temperature.

1 Serving: Calories 230 (Calories from Fat 80); Total Fat 9g (Saturated Fat 2g); Cholesterol 40mg; Sodium 240mg; Total Carbohydrate 34g (Dietary Fiber 0g); Protein 3g

Poppy seed can become rancid if it is stored for a long period in your cupboard. Stick it in your freezer, and it will keep almost forever.

chocolate lover's dream cake

Prep Time: 20 min ∎ **Start to Finish:** 3 hr 35 min ∎ 16 Servings

Cake

1 package butter recipe chocolate cake mix with
    pudding in the mix
$^1/_2$ cup chocolate milk
$^1/_3$ cup butter or margarine, melted
3 eggs
1 container (16 oz) sour cream
1 package (4-serving size) chocolate fudge instant
    pudding and pie filling mix
1 bag (12 oz) semisweet chocolate chips (2 cups)

Rich Chocolate Glaze

$^3/_4$ cup semisweet chocolate chips
3 tablespoons butter or margarine
3 tablespoons light corn syrup
$1^1/_2$ teaspoons water

1 Heat oven to 350°F. Generously grease 12-cup fluted tube cake pan with shortening; lightly flour.

2 In large bowl, mix cake mix, chocolate milk, butter, eggs, sour cream and pudding mix (dry) with spoon until well blended (batter will be very thick). Stir in chocolate chips. Spoon into pan.

3 Bake 55 to 65 minutes or until top springs back when touched lightly in center. Cool in pan 10 minutes. Turn pan upside down onto wire rack or heatproof serving plate; remove pan. Cool completely, about 2 hours.

4 In 1-quart saucepan, heat glaze ingredients over low heat, stirring frequently, until chocolate chips are melted and mixture is smooth. Drizzle glaze over cooled cake. Store loosely covered at room temperature.

1 Serving: Calories 460 (Calories from Fat 220); Total Fat 25g (Saturated Fat 13g); Cholesterol 75mg; Sodium 450mg; Total Carbohydrate 54g (Dietary Fiber 3g); Protein 5g

You don't want to lose even a drop of this divine batter, so measure the volume of your fluted tube cake pan using water to make sure it holds 12 cups. If the pan is smaller than 12 cups, the batter will overflow during baking.

double chocolate–cherry torte

Prep Time: 30 min ■ **Start to Finish:** 6 hr 35 min ■ 12 Servings

2 packages (8 oz each) semisweet baking chocolate, coarsely chopped

1 cup butter or margarine

6 eggs

1¹/₂ cups white chocolate chunks (from 12-oz bag)*

1¹/₂ cups whipping cream

4 oz cream cheese (from 8-oz package), softened

1 can (21 oz) cherry pie filling

¹/₄ teaspoon almond extract

2 tablespoons amaretto liqueur, if desired

1 Heat oven to 400°F. Spray bottom and side of 9-inch springform pan with cooking spray. In 3-quart saucepan, melt semisweet chocolate and butter over medium-low heat, stirring constantly, until smooth. Cool 30 minutes.

2 In medium bowl, beat eggs with electric mixer on high speed about 5 minutes or until about triple in volume. Fold into chocolate mixture. Pour into springform pan. Bake 15 to 20 minutes or until edge is set but center is still soft and jiggles slightly when moved. Cool completely in pan, about 1 hour 30 minutes. Then cover and refrigerate 1 hour 30 minutes.

3 In medium microwavable bowl, mix white chocolate and 2 tablespoons of the whipping cream. Microwave uncovered on High 20 to 40 seconds, stirring once, until chocolate is melted. Stir until well blended. In medium bowl, beat cream cheese on medium speed until smooth. Gradually add white chocolate mixture, beating until smooth. Add 1 cup of the pie filling; beat until well blended and cherries are broken up.

4 In another chilled medium bowl, beat remaining whipping cream and the almond extract on high speed until stiff peaks form. Fold in cherry chocolate mixture until well blended. Spread over dark chocolate layer. Refrigerate at least 2 hours but no longer than 48 hours.

5 In medium bowl, stir remaining pie filling and the liqueur until well blended. Remove side of springform pan. Serve torte topped with cherry sauce.

*You can use 1¹/₂ cups coarsely chopped white chocolate baking bars instead of the chunks.

1 Serving: Calories 680 (Calories from Fat 440); Total Fat 49g (Saturated Fat 27g); Cholesterol 190mg; Sodium 190mg; Total Carbohydrate 51g (Dietary Fiber 3g); Protein 8g

mud slide ice cream cake

Prep Time: 30 min ▪ **Start to Finish:** 6 hr ▪ 15 Servings

1 package chocolate fudge cake mix with pudding in the mix
1/2 cup butter or margarine, melted
2 eggs
2 tablespoons coffee-flavored liqueur or strong coffee
1 quart (4 cups) vanilla ice cream
1 container (12 oz) chocolate whipped ready-to-spread frosting
2 tablespoons coffee-flavored liqueur, if desired

1 Heat oven to 350°F. Grease bottom only of 13×9-inch pan with shortening or cooking spray.

2 In large bowl, mix cake mix, butter and eggs with spoon. Spread in pan. Bake 20 to 25 minutes or until center is set (top will appear dry and cracked). Cool completely, about 1 hour.

3 Brush 2 tablespoons liqueur over cake. Let ice cream stand about 15 minutes at room temperature to soften. Spread ice cream over cake. Freeze 3 hours or until firm.

4 In medium bowl, mix frosting and 2 tablespoons liqueur; spread over ice cream. Freeze at least 1 hour.

1 Serving: Calories 380 (Calories from Fat 160): Total Fat 18g (Saturated Fat 8g): Cholesterol 60mg: Sodium 400mg: Total Carbohydrate 51g (Dietary Fiber 2g): Protein 4g

Coffee lovers can substitute coffee-flavored ice cream for the vanilla.

index

Page numbers in *italics* indicate illustrations.